OUR JOURNEY WITH GOD

THE DOVE INTERNATIONAL STORY

LARRY & LAVERNE KREIDER

HOUSE TO HOUSE PUBLICATIONS

House To House Publications
Lititz, Pennsylvania USA
www.h2hp.com

Our Journey with God: The DOVE International Story
by Larry and LaVerne Kreider

Copyright © 2020 by DOVE International

Published by
House to House Publications
11 Toll Gate Road, Lititz, PA 17543 USA
Phone: 717.627.1996
www.h2hp.com

ISBN-978-0-9987574-7-6

Cover design by Malina Kongsynonh

DEDICATION

This book is dedicated to our Lord Jesus Christ,
to thousands of fellow believers in DOVE International
worldwide, and to all those who have served the
DOVE family during the past 40 years.

ACKNOWLEDGEMENTS

So many people were involved in this project, helping us to see this book become a reality. Lou Ann Good served as our writing assistant and interviewed dozens of people whose stories are in this book. Diane Omondi compiled and wrote many of the African stories. Both Diane and Lou Ann helped us bring the pieces of this global story together. A huge thank you to Sarah Sauder for her oversight of this project.

A special thank you to Keith Yoder who gave valuable insights and also wrote the foreword for the book.

A huge thank you to the DOVE International Apostolic Council team who have served with us and gave valuable insights and suggestions along the way to help make this book as accurate and life-giving as possible: Ron and Bonnie Myer, Peter Bunton, Craig and Tracie Nanna, Hesbone and Violet Odindo, Ibrahim and Diane Omondi, Steve and Mary Prokopchak, Brian and Janet Sauder, and Merle and Cheree Shenk.

A special thanks to Mervin Charles who gave valuable insights for this book regarding our early years as a church movement. A big thank you to Nancy Leatherman and Hillary Vargas for all of their proofreading and editing.

Thank you to everyone who gave their God stories during the past 40 years that are included in this book. And a huge thank you to the thousands of believers in the DOVE global family whose stories of their journey with God are not written in this book. You are true heroes.

CONTENTS

Our Journey with God

Foreword

I first met Larry and LaVerne when our paths crossed at a Christian retreat center in the early 1970s. Energetically, Larry engaged the youth that he will describe in the chronicle you are about to read. It was several years later before our paths converged again as we were seeking God's wisdom together in challenging times. Over the decades I have had the honor to join the story of DOVE as a teacher, mentor, advisor, and friend.

Throughout the account of passions, people, and places that follow, Larry has woven a tapestry of the character and culture of the DOVE family. His narrative exudes an enduring investment in youth, the power of encouragement and the inspiration of testimony. Also evident are the core commitments to small group ministry and spiritual parenting.

These vignettes of a world traveler show the dedication to international ministry and God-centered governance. Undergirded by sacrifice, generosity and prayer, the DOVE way of life has multiplied into a growing body of believers dedicated to the Great Commission of Christ.

Biblically, a generation is forty years. Like David who was commended for "serving the purpose of God in his generation," DOVE's story reveals how DOVE has pioneered and persevered in its generation as well as prepared the way for the next.

The pages that follow hold rich memories for those who have been part of DOVE's unfolding journey. Those who are observing this growing family of churches from outside-in will find valuable lessons shared with respectful transparency. As you turn these pages, you are witnessing the grace and faithfulness of God.

Keith Yoder, Ed. D., Founder,
Teaching the Word Ministries

Introduction

Writing this book was a team effort with dozens of faithful people providing significant insights that have shaped our journey. Looking back at our forty-plus years, we are humbled and amazed at the grace of God. We feel a bit like the children of Israel, who after seeing the hand of God defeat the Philistines set up a memorial, naming it Ebenezer, which means "thus far the Lord has helped us" (1 Samuel 7:12). Likewise, thus far, our God has helped the DOVE family.

Hundreds of people played key roles in the DOVE International family throughout our extraordinary journey. Some served in DOVE churches for a short time and some served for many years. Some of the original persons who helped birth our church family are still serving with us today. Others served as advisors. As time passed, some have gone to be with the Lord.

In some ways, this was a very difficult book to write. God has used so many people over the years in the DOVE story. We wanted to mention everyone by name, but we found this was impossible. We feel a bit like the writer of the book of John who said, "And there are also many other things that Jesus did, which if they were written one by one, I suppose that even the world itself could not contain the books that would be written" (John 21:25).

We are blessed and eternally grateful for every person who has been willing to serve with us. In times of abundance and in the hard times, we experienced the Lord's grace and His great blessing again and again. Together, the Lord has given an amazing inheritance to each of us.

I am grateful that LaVerne kept an accurate diary for more than fifty years. She took a few months to go over her diaries and glean stories that began years before our first Sunday morning service in October 1980. Without her detail in capturing these stories, we would not have remembered the specifics of many of the experiences God used to shape the DOVE family. I started this book project by chronicling the major events. Lou Ann Good was a great help as she also interviewed dozens of people who shared their memories and testimonies of God's faithfulness during the past 40 years. Both Lou Ann Good and Diane Omondi helped us bring the pieces of this story together.

We are aware that our story is written from our personal perspective and remembrance and from the viewpoint of those who were interviewed. Others could share insights and perspectives we have missed. This book has been written thematically and some accounts may therefore not follow an exact chronological description. Our desire is to write our story as accurately as possible and bring glory to God so that future generations can learn from both our mistakes and victories.

Enjoy the DOVE story of our journey with God.

God bless you!

Larry and LaVerne Kreider

CHAPTER 1

The "Back" Story

As LaVerne and I look back on the early days of the DOVE family, we recognize the seeds for the DOVE church movement were first planted in the summer of 1971. At that time, we were still single and involved in a youth group Bible study at Hammer Creek Mennonite Church near Lititz, Pennsylvania. Many of us in our youth group had recently surrendered our lives completely to the Lord and had a deep hunger for God.

As we studied the Scriptures together, we read in Acts 2:47 that people were coming to Christ daily. As believers on fire for God, we longed to see people coming to Christ every day in our generation. Located a few miles from our home was an at-risk community with limited opportunities in northern Lancaster County, Pennsylvania. It was scary for us, but our youth group took a step of faith to focus on this needy community because we wanted to make a difference in the lives of its young people.

We sensed the Lord calling us to build relationships with the youth of this community. We knew relationships are built by spending time together, so we designated every Tuesday night to play baseball with the teenagers who lived there.

One of the first people I met was a 13-year-old teenager who had no idea why there was an Easter or a Christmas.

We soon discovered that neither he nor many of the others in this community had ever been told that Jesus loved them and wanted a relationship with them. We were amazed that people living in what we considered to be a Bible belt had no knowledge of basic Bible truths. Jesus Christ was only a swear word to most of them.

Fire burned to spread God's love

A fire to spread God's love burned within us. Our small group learned the power of building friendships, which opened doors for us to share our faith in Christ. After our baseball outreaches each Tuesday night, we went to the home of our youth leaders to pray and hear the Lord's plan about how we could share Christ more effectively to this community.

Excitement at seeing God work built within our group. But the end of the summer brought changes. LaVerne and I got married. We bid farewell to our friends and spent the next year as stateside missionaries on John's Island, South Carolina. Although we missed the youth outreach, it continued with a team from the Hammer Creek Mennonite Church youth group.

A year later, LaVerne and I returned to Lancaster County to help my father on the family farm. We reconnected with the youth outreach. Eventually the team rented a house to establish a place for young people to hang out with us. We offered crafts, cooking, sports, a coffee house night and a Bible study for those who wanted to learn about Christianity. One by one, a few of these teenagers gave their lives to Christ. We were thrilled.

Witnessing the teens responding to the love of Jesus fired our passion to spend even more time reaching unchurched kids. One of those was Norma Spangler Denlinger who can still recall all the team leaders by name. "I remember playing baseball in our backyard, craft night…almost every night something was going on," she said. "They treated us like family. I remember being taught to drive a car by one of the women. Activities together built trust into our relationships."

LaVerne's cousin Linford Good taught a Bible study for those interested in knowing more about Christianity, but the new believers also needed a Bible study designed to help them grow in their newfound faith. I was asked by our team to start a Bible study each Tuesday night for the new believers. LaVerne and I had learned about Paul-Timothy mentoring relationships when we were missionaries. We decided to try this concept with the new believers. Of her assigned mentor, Norma recalls, "We studied the Bible, prayed and had long talks together."

Within a few years, dozens of young people came to faith in Christ. Our outreach group formed a non-profit organization called Lost but Found. Volunteer staff from various churches joined us. We also started similar outreach ministries to reach unchurched youth in the villages of Hopeland and Rothsville and eventually in other communities throughout the area. New believers came to the Bible study on Tuesday nights from these various Lost but Found outreaches. Donna (Garman) Esbenshade, one of the unchurched youth reached through the Hopeland Lost but Found, remembers those early years with fondness.

"Larry and LaVerne and the other leaders modeled God's love," Donna says. "It was the love of God that drew me to attend the Tuesday night Bible study taught by Larry. He really instilled a love for the Word. He handed out notebooks and encouraged us to take notes. I still have that notebook and remember the first lesson he taught: 'Resist the devil and he will flee from you. Draw nigh to God and he will draw nigh to you.'"

Initially we thought only ordained pastors could baptize new believers. So we asked one of our Lost but Found board members who was an ordained pastor to baptize the new believers in a local creek. He did this willingly, but the next time we had new converts who wanted to be baptized, he told us we should baptize them ourselves. He said the Scriptures are clear that neither Jesus nor Paul baptized many people; most baptisms were done by the early disciples. After that explanation, we started baptizing new believers in local creeks, swimming pools, horse troughs and bathtubs—wherever we could find enough water. Today we continue to encourage small group leaders and small group members to baptize those who come to Christ.

Searching for a spiritual family

Involvement grew in the Tuesday evening Bible study. We really believed it was important for the new believers to become part of a local church. Sunday church services had always been a vital part of our lives, and we believed each of these new believers needed to be a part of a spiritual family.

Our home church, where LaVerne's father, brother, and uncle were the pastors, was a wonderful church, but the youth from unchurched backgrounds did not fit into the structure of this established church. Determined to find a church for the new believers, we drove van loads of new believers to other local church services each weekend. In those days, most churches had both Sunday morning and Sunday night services. On Sunday nights, we visited Baptist, Assembly of God, Independent, Bible Fellowship, Methodist, Mennonite,

New believers were baptized in a local creek.

and all types and flavors of churches. Sometimes we brought more new believers to a Sunday night service than the number of members present.

After the services, the van loads of young people returned to our house. We worshipped God as I played my guitar. We prayed, counseled and built relationships together. Our team saw afresh that these young Christians loved God and wanted to grow in the knowledge of God, but no matter what churches we visited, the group members did not seem to fit into the established congregations.

Jesus people

These were the days when God was moving among a young generation across the United States. In what is remembered as the Jesus Movement, record numbers of youth and young adults surrendered their lives to Jesus. Miracles of instantaneous deliverance from drugs and baptisms of the Holy Spirit became daily occurrences. Like many leaders, we were perplexed when reports reached us that many "Jesus people" were also having difficulty fitting into established churches. Without teaching and oversight, some of the "Jesus people" were falling back into sinful lifestyles.

We did not want this to happen to the new Christians who were a part of our outreach. As I was praying about this, the Lord spoke to me one day and asked, "Are you willing to be involved with the underground church?"

In those days, the underground church was identified with horrific accounts of Christians being persecuted for their faith in Russia and in other Communist nations. Christians in these countries gathered to worship in secret in order to avoid being imprisoned, tortured, and killed. I wrestled with God. I wept. I hated the thought of persecution. But I finally surrendered and promised the Lord I was willing to do whatever He was asking me to do.

In 1979 I started a small discipleship and accountability group with a few friends, and we soon invited our wives and others from the Bible study to join us. This was our first small group. We called it a house fellowship.

Sometime later we began to understand more about what God meant when He asked me to be involved in the "underground church." Consider a tree: it has bark, branches, leaves, and fruit above the ground. But that is only the part of the tree we can see. It is the unseen root system that nourishes the tree and determines the vibrancy of the leaves, fruit, and branches. If the root system is strong and healthy, the tree remains healthy. If the root system shrivels, becomes root-bound and decays, the effects will be seen above ground in the blighted leaves, decaying branches, and peeling bark.

Understanding the underground church

I began to understand that the underground church is likewise representative of the root system of the church. In Acts 20:20, Paul taught the believers publicly and from house to house. The New Testament church met in relational small groups and made disciples "underground" from house to house and also met in larger meetings in the temple courts. Our traditions told us the Sunday morning church services were the most important part of a local church, but we found the house fellowship to be the place where we were experiencing the most spiritual growth.

When believers are nourished and healthy in these small underground groups, the whole church becomes stronger. As water and nutrients feed the tree by coming up through the root system, so the church is nourished and strengthened by what happens in the unseen realm of church life—believers being discipled and growing through their involvement in "underground" small groups or house churches.

Our main focus was on Christ, not a program

We saw the necessity for each believer to grow in their relationship with Christ. We believed our main focus should be making disciples as Jesus taught us, not a Sunday morning church program. We were convinced God's purpose for our outreach ministry team was to train youth to grow in the Word of God. Since this was done most effectively one-on-one in Paul-Timothy relationships and in small group Bible studies, we called this the underground part of the church.

In small group gatherings, believers learn to know each other, care for each other, and be aware of each other's concerns. We challenged one another to reach those who do not know Christ, and we prayed for each other more intimately than we could in the larger gatherings of Sunday morning or Sunday evening services.

Our realization that we needed to start a different type of church for new believers and not force them to become part of the established churches was later clarified when a Men-

Larry and LaVerne in the early days.

nonite bishop explained the meaning of Matthew 9:16, 17: "No one puts a piece of unshrunk cloth on an old garment; for the patch pulls away from the garment, and the tear is made worse. Nor do they put new wine into old wineskins, or else the wineskins break, the wine is spilled, and the wineskins are ruined. But they put new wine into new wineskins, and both are preserved."

He explained that a wineskin is like a balloon. It needs to be flexible and pliable. Putting a new Christian into an old structure can cause the structure to break, and the new Christian may be lost. New Christians should be placed in new structures that are flexible and that encourage spiritual growth.

Our team realized we had been trying to force new believers (or new wine) into older church structures (old wineskins). The older church structures were wonderful for the people who served there for many years, but the new believers we led to Christ were not fitting into this structure. They needed a new type of church, a new structure, a new wineskin. What better place than a home? We repeatedly saw that new believers thrived in small group Bible studies. They prayed for each other, saw God move among them, listened attentively to teaching, asked questions, and grew in Christ.

Rhema Bible study

This did not mean that we did not encourage larger group gatherings. In 1979 I had started a new youth teaching ministry with my friend Melvin Landis. We called it Rhema, which means "the word the Holy Spirit quickens to a specific person for a specific situation." The Rhema Bible study replaced the former youth Bible study that I had been leading in our home. I and several other outreach members had been baptized (filled) with the Holy Spirit and started to minister differently than we had in the past. We believed God for healing and miracles. Each week young men and women submitted to the lordship of Christ and were filled with the Holy Spirit. The Rhema Bible study quickly attracted more than one hundred youth and young adults each week.

Both Lost but Found and Rhema Youth Ministries focused on evangelism. Rhema sent evangelism teams into a local mall and handed out brochures with testimonies of lives transformed by Christ. Lost but Found focused on friendship evangelism by establishing new outreaches in various towns in our area.

A second house fellowship

The house fellowship continued to grow so our house was no longer large enough to contain all the young people attending. In January 1980, a second house fellowship began in Don and Jeanette Weaver's home. Members of the first house fellowship continued meeting in the homes of Luis and Karen Ruiz and Phil and Doris Martin. (Both Jeanette and Karen are LaVerne's sisters.)

On a February 1980 Sunday morning, LaVerne and I were sitting in a church pew at Hammer Creek Mennonite Church. Between the time of Sunday School and the main church service, the Holy Spirit spoke to me: "I have called you to start something new." At the end of the service, a friend told me about a group of Mennonite mission leaders who were looking for people to start new churches. He encouraged me to attend a meeting that week. I did. The mission leaders encouraged me to continue building a team to start a new church. This was my confirmation from the Lord about the call I was sensing to start something new—a church.

A season of intense prayer developed. Some of us had read the book *Revival Lectures* by Charles Finney, and we were hungry for revival. We wanted to experience more of God in our lives. Although there had been seasons of revival in our area in the past, we longed to experience ongoing revival. Our nucleus of house fellowship members had night watches of prayer where one of us prayed for an hour and then called the next person on the list to pray. We did this night after night. During 1979 and 1980 we also had prayer and intercession every Sunday night.

Rhema meetings thrived. Each week was exciting as teen-agers and those in their early twenties gave their lives completely to the lordship of Christ and received the baptism in the Holy Spirit. Some of these young people are still active in DOVE today. Sarah Mohler (Sauder), was only sixteen when she first attended Rhema Youth Ministries at the old Ephrata Mennonite Church building. She continues to lead our publications ministry nearly forty years later. Brian Sauder was seventeen when he first attended the Rhema Bible study. After college graduation, Brian served as the DOVE youth director and later as a church overseer. Since 1995, he also has been a DOVE International Apostolic Team member. Brian's wife, Janet, was involved in both Lost but Found and Rhema as a teenager, and before marrying Brian, was part of DOVE's first missionary outreach to Scotland.

After the Lord spoke to me about starting something new, I invited some leaders who were involved in our house fellowships, in Rhema, and in Lost but Found to join me. Some of these leaders did not feel called to help start a new church, so they continued with these ministries. Core members and other people who were interested in helping establish a church for new believers began meeting at 5:00 a.m. on Saturday mornings for prayer. We often met on Sunday afternoons as well.

A mutual friend introduced us to Mervin and Laurel Charles, who became key leaders with us. Most of those who joined in this new venture were those whom we had relationship with and who were serving with us already. But none of us had any idea what lay ahead. We were just ready to obey God.

CHAPTER 2

DOVE is Born

On October 12, 1980, about twenty-five people met for our first public meeting on a Sunday morning in the house at Abundant Living Ministries near Brickerville, Pennsylvania. Abundant Living Ministries was a dynamic marriage and counselling ministry operated by Mervin Charles's parents, Norman and Betty Charles. We met at Abundant Living weekly for Sunday morning celebration meetings, but our main focus was the groups meeting from house to house during the week. By that time, we had three house fellowship groups meeting "underground."

In those early years, house churches were rare in our area. We pioneered through the uncharted territory of determining how to start house fellowships and also conduct a Sunday meeting that encouraged and motivated believers to live wholeheartedly for God.

We had decided that six couples should serve together in leadership. At first, we thought that no one person should lead the team. This team leadership approach seemed to work to a point. If one leader felt led to share a message, the others supported him. But this approach also brought challenges. At times, several people felt led to share a message; at other times, no one took the initiative to preach. Perhaps that happened because a leader did not want to seem too audacious or preferred to give another leader the opportunity to teach. But it began to lead to stress and confusion. One Sunday morning no one preached because we were unable to decide who should preach. Consequently, those in our church encouraged us serving on the leadership team to get clarity regarding leadership and decision-making in order to bring stability to our new church.

We searched for clarification. We learned years later in a book authored by Harold Eberle, *The Complete Wineskin*[1], "After observing many churches, I can personally tell you that no matter what form of government a church claims to have, there is always one person who openly or quietly holds the greatest influence over the church. Setting up proper government is never a matter of keeping it out of the hands of one person but putting it into the hands of God's person."

Building our team

We realized we needed leadership among our team, and Mervin Charles and I were appointed as overseers of the house fellowships and of the new church. I was chosen as the apostolic leader responsible for overseeing and implementing ministry, and Mervin was chosen as the prophetic support leader. We were called the overseers of DOVE Christian Fellowship.

"As co-ministers, their strengths merged to form a strong cord. Larry's visionary dynamic, bold exhortations, and Mervin's calm, logical, and sequential explanation of scriptures fed the growing body of believers," recalls a member.

Having designated these roles of leadership did not mean team leadership was not valued. It was understood that each person had gifts that would contribute toward the spiritual growth of the group. One of the main teachings at DOVE continues to be that every believer is called to be a minister and serve others according to Ephesians 4:11-12: "And He Himself gave some to be apostles, some prophets, some evangelists, and some pastors and teachers, for the equipping of the saints (the believers) for the work of ministry, for the edifying of the body of Christ." Simply stated, all believers are equipped by leadership to minister.

We learned that all believers have various gifts from God to use to minister to one another. And there are people among us who have the leadership gifts of apostle, prophet, evangelist, pastor, and teacher who are called by God to equip us to minister the life of Christ to those in our families, our cell groups, and those we meet in daily life. We call these leaders the fivefold ministry: the gift of apostle, prophet, evangelist, pastor, and teacher.

Leading as a servant

Servant leadership became very important to us. Servant leadership means each person is valued, no one is above the other, and each is willing to serve wherever needed. For example, in the early days I preached the Word one week and served in children's ministry the next week.

Core members Phil and Doris Martin remember those early years. Doris says, "We saw the need to mentor new believers. I started mentoring several girls who had come from unchurched backgrounds. Reaching out to others impacted our lives with new vision and zeal."

Another member, Marty, was a shy teenager who babysat for neighbors occasionally. One day she received a call from a neighbor she had never met. The woman had been given Marty's name by another neighbor who recommended Marty as a babysitter. When Marty learned that the woman, Jan Dorward, was Jewish, she was eager to introduce her to Jesus. She told Jan she had someone she wanted her to meet. Marty introduced us to Jan, who was skeptical of Christians and considered herself agnostic. Jan was amazed to hear me explain Old Testament Scriptures that foretold the coming of Jesus. That same evening, she accepted Jesus as her Lord and Savior. Jan and her husband began attending the second house fellowship and joined us when we started our first Sunday morning gathering. Within the small groups, salvations such as Jan's sparked excitement for sharing Jesus.

Naming our new church

Our new church needed a name. One weekend some of the core members including Mervin and Laurel Charles, Don and Jeanette Weaver, Phil and Doris Martin, Luis and Karen Ruiz, Galen and Jolie Hershey, and LaVerne and I went to a cabin to pray specifically for a name for our new church.

Many possibilities were discussed. Jeanette Weaver saw in prayer a vision of a banner being unfurled with the letters D.O.V.E. She submitted her entry to a list of potential names and from this list, four were selected for a vote. When DOVE was not listed as one of the four possibilities, Jeanette was stunned. Heart pounding, Jeanette bravely forged ahead to share details that she did not initially share with the group. D.O.V.E. was an acronym, she believed. This revelation brought unity because the name "Declaring Our Victory Emmanuel" aptly described the purpose of the new outreach. D.O.V.E. (Declaring Our Victory Emmanuel) was soon referred to as DOVE Christian Fellowship. (We called it a fellowship, not a church in those early years).

Our first logo

By the end of November 1980, we moved the church to the lower level of the barn at Abundant Living. About fifty people attended the first service in the barn. We had started with three house fellowships meeting during the week on Wednesday evenings, but we sensed the three house fellowships were not experiencing the unity needed in order to move ahead together. Consequently, the three house fellowships were reduced to two house fellowships, one led by Mervin and one led by me. We found that when we were in unity, God promised to command His blessing and the house fellowships began to multiply.

Our three main focuses were prayer, evangelism, and discipleship. We called it our three-legged stool that would be stable in any setting. Prayer was vital, we believed. We continued to seek God for revival and held many all-night prayer meetings, sometimes praying for the fellowship and other times for Rhema Youth Ministries or Lost but Found. Sometimes we prayed for all three. We prayed for laborers for the harvest and for new believers who needed a new church. But we also focused on evangelism and on making disciples after the pattern of Jesus.

Throughout the past forty years, prayer and fasting has become an extremely important discipline for us. For we realize that in every situation, we urgently need God. We have had late-night prayer meetings, all-night prayer meetings, early morning prayer meetings, 24/7 prayer, and personal prayer we sometimes call meeting God in the secret place. Extraordinary prayer has been vital for us to stay tuned to hear the voice of God.

While the new church was birthed and began to grow, we continued to focus on reaching youth and young adults for the Lord through both Lost but Found and Rhema Youth Ministries Bible studies.

An on-ramp for the church

I worked with Jerry Horst to start a second Rhema Youth Ministry Bible study at Our Barn in New Danville, south of Lancaster City. Both the Ephrata and the New Danville ministries were like an on-ramp for young people who were getting right with God and needed a new local church. In the next few years, Lost but Found and Rhema Youth Ministries began to work together under one non-profit ministry, Rhema Youth Ministries, and we dropped the name "Lost but Found."

Later, a third Rhema was started in Manheim, Pennsylvania. The youth ministry continued to grow.

From the beginning of our house fellowships, both men and women were placed in ministry. Scriptures affirm that God uses both men and women as leaders. Priscilla and Aquila worked together as a team (Romans 16:3). Priscilla may even have been the one giving leadership to the people God placed within her spiritual care while her husband supported her. Our team believed that husbands and wives have unique gifts but should affirm each other's call to serve. Many times, one spouse is more verbal than the other, but the quieter one often works diligently behind the scenes and each complements the other as they flow in unity.

Mervin and I spent a lot of time praying together in those days. Each of our hearts were really open to the Lord, and when needed, we discussed differences and walked in love. God gave us grace to make wise decisions. We were influenced by Larry Tomczak and C.J. Mahaney who led a new church called Gathering of Believers in Washington D.C., and by Bob Weiner and other leaders from Maranatha Ministries, a college church-planting ministry.

The Lord constantly brought people into the DOVE family who eventually became dynamic leaders within DOVE. About this time, we had a visit from a young Kenyan university student, Ibrahim Omondi, who was studying at Goshen College in Indiana. He was looking for churches in the USA that were using small home groups as a vital part of their church. He heard about DOVE Christian Fellowship and decided to visit us. Our hearts connected as we met to pray. Little did we know the blessing of this friendship that is ongoing nearly forty years later, or how it would bring great blessing and advancement to God's kingdom in the nations.

Although DOVE Christian Fellowship had grown to one hundred people at this point, no leader was receiving financial support. I continued to juggle working on the farm, leading the church and participating in Rhema Youth Ministries. With the many new people coming into the fellowship, we saw the need to focus on training and mentoring leaders. On a regular basis, I met with the men who were leaders of the house fellowships and LaVerne met with the women leaders.

The leadership team discussed financial support for my family and decided to take an offering twice a month and believe God with us for support. In June 1981, I officially left my job on the family farm to give full focus to the new church plant.

In September 1981, I taught the first teaching in a series on the subject "Jesus Christ as Lord." Many years later, this series developed into a set of booklets to help new believers understand the basic foundations of the Christian life. The Biblical Foundation series continues to be used today in many nations and has been translated into several languages to help establish biblical truth in the lives of believers.

The new DOVE Christian Fellowship church and Rhema Youth Ministries began to work more closely together. We often had prayer meetings together, and we continued to experience a move of the Holy Spirit in the celebration gatherings.

Soon Sunday morning attendance filled the lower part of the barn at Abundant Living Ministries, forcing us to find a larger space to meet. Plans were made to renovate the upper part of the barn at Abundant Living for our growing fellowship. Until that was completed, we found a place at the Lititz Area Mennonite School to house our growing congregation in May of 1982. While there, DOVE continued to grow.

Merv Charles served as a key leader in our early days.

A new house fellowship was started in Ephrata and another house fellowship was established in Lebanon County. Ron and Bonnie Myer first came to DOVE Christian Fellowship at the Lititz Area Mennonite School and quickly became part of the new Lebanon County house fellowship. We had no idea at that time how much the Lord would use the Myer family in the DOVE global family. Forty years later, Ron continues as the assistant international director of the DOVE International Apostolic Team. (More on Ron and Bonnie's story later).

Some of our house fellowships were Rhema groups and others were DOVE groups. Since I was in leadership in both ministries, it seemed to work. But as the workload increased, a visionary team, which included Mervin and Laurel Charles, Jerry and Sue Horst, Jay and Linda Good, Melvin and Nancy Landis, Fred and Marilyn Wiegand, and LaVerne and me, formed and focused on overseeing our growing ministries. From its beginning until 1987, the visionary team was greatly influential and deeply committed to the vision of both Rhema and DOVE. Although Mervin and I were the overseers of DOVE, the visionary team gave more and more input into both Rhema and DOVE, which grew more closely connected.

We also started another Rhema meeting at Abundant Living that we called Brickerville Rhema. Initially it was mostly attended by youth from our new church but soon grew to include those from the region who were hungry for God. Although he was just a young boy, Merle Shenk sometimes came along to the Rhema Bible studies with his older siblings. He was probably the youngest person who ever came to Rhema. Merle is now a lead pastor in the DOVE family and a member of the DOVE International Apostolic Council.

The church had now grown to 250 people, which amazed LaVerne and me. In the beginning of DOVE, we had talked about the future of the church and believed that if the church grew to 200 people by the time we were eighty years of age, that would be awesome. But we soon realized that God's plans were different than ours. Originally, we had wanted the church to be an outreach for the unchurched only, but more and more believers were coming to our celebration services and house fellowships. These people were hungry to participate in a church operating in relational Christianity, exercising the gifts of the Holy Spirit, and reaching out to the unsaved.

Our team ministered to dozens of young people weekly.

We needed more leaders for our small groups and for the growing ministry. We prayed for two types of people to come to DOVE: new believers and laborers to help with the harvest.

Teacher training classes for house fellowship leaders were established. Four potential leaders received training together at each session. Participants watched a video I taught called "Teaching with Confidence." This was followed by a short three-minute scriptural teaching on a cassette tape (yes, we had cassette tapes in those days). Participants then took a short time to study notes, personalize the teaching and teach into a video camera. The participants watched the video of their own teaching to critique and improve their delivery. Sometimes a whole day was designated to train groups of four at a time on how to teach practical Christian living from the Scriptures.

Sharing responsibilities

By November 1982, 270 people were attending our Sunday morning services. As the ministry expanded, it became clear to LaVerne and me that we needed to release more responsibilities to others. Mervin Charles was helping with much of the counseling and took on other leadership responsibilities. Mervin was able to eventually move on from his job and was supported by the church. But it was the house fellowship leaders who did most of the personal ministry and discipleship. LaVerne and I also examined our schedules to see if we needed to make some changes. We recognized the necessity to establish a personal family day each week and designated Thursdays as that day.

LaVerne sensed that her call to mentor leaders' wives was more important than heading up committees and planning women's events. She said, "In my times of prayer, I knew what God had called me to do. It was clear: train a few women at a time." She poured her life into a few of the women who were small group leaders in the church. The relationships she developed took time and effort. She inquired about their marriages and families. She prayed and wept with them as they went through difficult seasons and rejoiced with them when they experienced life's joys.

Many in leadership were young married couples with young children. Finding a balance between ministry and family was essential. We had been taught this when Paul Johansson from Elim Bible College came to minister to our Rhema group, DOVE Christian Fellowship, and to our leaders. Paul had spent years as a missionary in Africa before being appointed president of Elim Bible College in Lima, New York. Before he left, I asked him for any input or concern and he advised, "Larry, you don't need to die for the church; Jesus already died for the church. Your responsibility is to die for your wife."

Paul's advice continues to impact me today. 1 Timothy 5:8 confirms, "Those who won't care for their relatives, especially those in their own household, have denied the faith. Such people are worse than unbelievers." Our spouses and families are precious gifts from the Father and need to be a priority.

Although many of those in our new church were single, we encouraged healthy relationships for both singles and husbands and wives. "The best gift you can give your children is to love their mother," we taught the young husbands. When children see their dads demonstrating loving actions toward their mothers, it builds security within them and strengthens the home. Another example of how we encouraged couples regarding the importance of valuing each other was by conducting DOVE marriage events where many husbands and wives renewed their marriage vows.

Encouraging leaders

Building relationships through hospitality was always a huge part of our lives. In our home, LaVerne and I hosted hot dog roasts, dinners and homemade ice cream socials for as many as fifty-five leaders at a time. When our church continued to grow, we held appreciation dinners for house fellowship leaders at local restaurants. The first house fellowship leaders' retreat at Camp Andrews registered about 120 people. We recognized the importance of valuing our small group leaders.

Monthly training meetings were conducted for house fellowship leaders. Every other month, men and women met together for small group leaders training, and the next month women and men met separately for training and encouragement. At the women's gatherings, LaVerne taught women to be supportive of each other and not envious. She bound the spirit of comparison that was often prevalent among women. Her bubbly, loving, and encouraging personality reflected her belief that as a leader, she sees herself beneath others pushing them upwards towards God instead of being above them. Her positive, encouraging attitude breathed vitality and love among the women. LaVerne taught them to rejoice in God's provision and be more than a conqueror in every area where God had placed them.

Learning from other ministries

We were always seeking to learn from other ministries that God was blessing. We attended a Mennonite church planting conference each year in the early years. At these Mennonite church planting conferences, we met others throughout our nation who were planting new churches. This was very encouraging for us.

We were influenced by major ministries in our nation and visited many of them. In those beginning years, we had many speakers from Maranatha Ministries, a college campus outreach, speak at our church. We attended their annual leadership training conferences. We learned from Maranatha that young people can be called to the "ministry of helps" to serve leaders

A home fellowship meets to study God's word, pray and reach the lost.

and their families so the leaders had more time for ministry. When Lavern Martin, a young man in our new church, saw this, he asked if he could serve in this way. I hesitated with this idea for some time, but eventually told him if he was sure it was an instruction from the Lord, he could do it. In his spare time, Lavern helped me in practical ways and assisted me on Sunday mornings with behind-the-scenes administration. It was a great blessing! Charlene Hoover also helped us with our children, giving LaVerne and me more time to minister to people. She even travelled with us overseas to Scotland when we ministered there.

We invited well-known charismatic speakers to our fellowship at DOVE and at the Rhema gatherings. These included Gerald Derstine, Winkie Pratney, Tommy Reid, Paul Johansson, Larry Tomczak and CJ Mahaney, Bob Weiner, Rice Broocks, and others from Maranatha Ministries. Dick Iversen from Bible Temple in Oregon and Dick Benjamin from Anchorage, Alaska, were each overseeing a movement of churches touching the nations, and they also came to speak into our lives and fellowship. Dick Iverson had learned how to incorporate the prophetic into their ministry and this really helped us. Francis Anfuso from Christian Equippers International taught us how to evangelize using the "Two-Question Test." Satish Raiborde, from Nagpur, India, taught us much about faith.

Although we learned much from other ministries, at times some of it became a distraction from our own vision. Sometimes we fell into the trap of adopting methods that worked for other churches even though the Lord had not called us to use those same methods. Eventually, we recognized that we needed to follow God's call on our lives and not be pushed into a style that did not fit us. David tried on Saul's armor, but it did not fit. Likewise, we cannot wear someone else's "armor" and expect it to fit. How true this became for our fledgling church. We learned the hard way that it is of utmost importance to hear from the Lord for the direction to take as a church.

International connections

In that era, opportunities to connect with international ministries were rare. We weren't particularly seeking international connections, but they happened. In retrospect, we can see how God's hand was directing from the beginning for DOVE to become an international church movement.

For example, David Brett, who had started YWAM in Scotland, spoke at one of our Rhema celebrations. This contact opened the door for us to eventually go to Scotland with our first overseas mission team.

We sensed we could learn much from overseas ministries that often experienced miracles and hundreds of salvations. Juan Carlos Ortiz from Argentina was one of our speakers, and we designated his book *Disciple* as required reading for our leaders. We also made the book *Successful Home Cell Groups* by Dr. David Yonggi Cho in Korea required reading for leaders.

Mervin Charles and I went to hear Pastor Cho, who led the world's largest church, at a meeting in New Jersey. We made the decision to go to Korea to experience the largest church in the world. A few months later, LaVerne and I traveled to Korea with Mervin and Laurel Charles and Jerry and Sue Horst to learn how the Korean church experienced phenomenal growth. While there, we experienced a fresh passion for prayer as we witnessed the diligence among the Korean believers.

In response to Pastor Cho's example, we stopped using the term "house fellowships" and began calling our small groups "cell churches" or "cell groups." Because our physical bodies

Jerry and Sue Horst, Merv and Laurel Charles and Larry and LaVerne traveled to Korea to learn more about cell groups.

are made up of cells that multiply and grow during the healthy process of mitosis, the name "cell" was adopted to signify that spiritual health is similarly represented by smaller units, cells, that grow and multiply in the Body of Christ.

We taught that ministries such as water baptisms, communion, praying for the sick, and personal ministry should happen in cell groups. We believed the saints (the believers) were the ministers (Ephesians 4:11, 12). The house fellowship was the church meeting underground, and we emphasized the need for everyone to be involved in that part of the church. We called our Sunday meetings "celebrations," because in them we celebrated what Jesus was doing in the cell groups throughout the week. We encouraged each other to recognize we do not "go to church." We are the church.

Although we had many well-known speakers minister at our events, we knew that extravagant church programs and famous speakers could never take the place of personal relationships formed in genuine community. Personal testimonies, messages in tongues and interpretation, and prophetic messages were the norm in both corporate celebrations and in cell meetings.

Experiencing God's grace

We struggled at times in these early days with certain doctrines that caused disagreements. DOVE taught a strong grace message, emphasizing God can use trials in our lives to mold us into His image because of His amazing grace. Those who had focused on only strong faith teaching at that time believed that if we fully trusted God, nothing bad should happen to us. But we taught that we live in a fallen world where difficult things can happen to us at times. The good news is that God redeems His people and gives us His grace to turn what Satan meant for evil into good.

Mennonite connection

Back in 1980, as we were praying about beginning a new church for youth and young believers, Mervin and I had sought counsel from Paul Landis who was the president of Eastern Mennonite Missions and a Mennonite bishop with Lancaster Mennonite Conference. We desired accountability from a more mature church leader open to the work of the Holy Spirit. He surprised us, though, by taking our request to the Bishop Board of the Mennonite Conference. We met with the Bishop Board Executive Committee and the entire bishop board. They didn't know what to do with us, but God provided direction through a visiting Christian leader, Daniel Yutsy, who grew up Amish but was at that time a professor at Taylor University in Indiana. He met with the executive committee and with Mervin Charles and me. After a meaningful but brief interaction he turned to the bishops and said, "Just release them and let them go." And the bishops affirmed us.

Paul Landis, along with another local bishop, Paul Hollinger, served as our oversight and counsel. God used them greatly, including in a time of crisis that emerged in our first year when we needed to discern how to have clear leadership among our leadership team. We are so grateful for them. We sensed a need to be able to perform weddings, so both Mervin and I were licensed for ministry by the Mennonite church in May 1981 and ordained a year later in May 1982.

Although DOVE was not a Mennonite church, we participated in some of the Mennonite conferences. For example, nineteen men from DOVE and Rhema traveled to New Jersey to a church planters' conference sponsored by Eastern Mennonite Missions. We later hosted a church planters' conference for the Eastern Mennonite Missions churches at Abundant Living with Rice Broocks from Maranatha Ministries as the speaker.

In 1984, the Mennonite Church asked us to make a decision: either formally join the Lancaster Conference as a Mennonite congregation or no longer have ordinations through them. This news came to us just as Mervin Charles and I were ready to leave on a mission trip to Mexico and Guatemala.

One morning while in Guatemala City in our host pastor's home, I sensed God guiding me in the decision we needed to make. Galatians 4 speaks of an heir being "subject to guardians and trustees until the time set by his father." I shared the scripture with Mervin. Both of us realized we had been blessed by the relationship and oversight of the Mennonite Church and bishops, but we were now to move forward in the timing God had set.

Although we loved and appreciated the Mennonites, we made the decision to no longer be ordained by the Mennonite Church. We had so many in our church who did not have a Mennonite background. We felt the Lord leading us to establish a new entity. On November 5, Mervin and I typed the notice informing the whole congregation that we had decided not to continue our involvement with the Mennonite Church. We started our own ordination process.

During this time, we saw a continual move of the Holy Spirit at Rhema Youth Ministries and at DOVE celebrations. God was blessing us, and we saw no need for outside accountability. Later, we realized it was a mistake not to appoint spiritual fathers and mothers or advisors outside of DOVE to oversee us and mentor us. This caused some major problems about ten years later, which will be explained later. But at the time, our new church was filled with excitement. We poured our energies into spreading the gospel at every opportunity.

Seven-county vision

God spoke to us about reaching a seven-county region in south central Pennsylvania. We talked and prayed about this constantly: God called us to Lancaster, Lebanon, York, Berks, Schuylkill, Dauphin, and Chester Counties. These counties were our areas of focus. We constantly prayed over maps of these seven counties. An air of expectancy for God to do great things permeated the atmosphere.

New believers were taught basic biblical principles such as salvation, water baptism, Holy Spirit baptism, giving and receiving forgiveness, and the call to fulfill the Great Commission by making disciples. Believers in our church gladly shared the good news of Jesus Christ with others. Transformation happened in the lives of many who desired to grow deeper in the Lord.

Television ministry begins

In April 1985, a speaker came from Maranatha Ministries to share at Rhema Youth Ministries and was videotaped for our new television ministry called Rhema Celebration. We broadcast this on the local Christian TV station. This started our journey to television broadcasts every Saturday night and eventually on Sunday for many years. Jerry Horst and Brian Sauder worked together to produce the shows. In addition to editing and directing, they organized fundraisers to attain money for the needed equipment.

Initially Jerry Horst and I hosted the TV show. Some years later, Duane Britton joined us on the show as a host. The television ministry needed crisis counselors, so we set up a 24-hour crisis counseling schedule and paid some of the crisis counselors by the hour. We called this ministry RCTV and we recorded special events that we hosted, such as when Frances Anfuso taught spirit-led evangelism courses. The format changed over the years as the producers interviewed people in the public eye such as a NASCAR racer and contemporary Christian musicians. In the 1990s, RCTV changed from a non-profit to a for-profit company that operated under the RCTV board. Don Barley, who attended the Manheim Rhema Bible study and had become a full-time employee in RCTV's early years, continues to direct this company today.

Youth ministry flourishes

As the Rhema outreaches grew, this ministry to youth required a lot of time. We began to call for more workers to reach high schools and help with these outreaches. A group of believers from the Hamburg, Pennsylvania, area had been filled with the Holy Spirit and were desiring to connect with a church that focused on the supernatural and on evangelism.

Larry and Duane Britton on the Rhema Celebration TV set.

They joined the DOVE family. Others became active in teaching at high school outreaches and youth events. Maranatha Ministries developed a Rock and Roll Seminar that was presented as an evangelism tool. As part of our evangelistic outreach, several DOVE leaders learned how to teach the Rock and Roll Seminar and presented it at local events and abroad. When our first overseas mission team went to Scotland, we taught the Rock and Roll Seminar at a school in Peterhead, Scotland.

Various high school clubs allowed us to teach from the Bible and share our God stories. We ministered in high schools throughout the greater Lancaster area and prayed for students to receive the lordship of Christ and be filled with the Holy Spirit. After a few years, we became so involved in caring for our growing church that we no longer focused as much on high school ministry.

DOVE leadership helped Abundant Living Ministries teach a seminar for pastoral couples. Duane and Reyna Britton, who at that point pastored New Life Fellowship in Reading, Pennsylvania, attended the seminar where a long-term relationship was kindled that continues until this day. In 1987 the Brittons became part of the then recent church plant called DOVE Lebanon/Berks Celebration. Later, the Brittons served with DOVE in Kenya for two years before Duane's installment as the lead elder for DOVE Westgate. For more than 30 years, the Brittons have served in various capacities in the DOVE International family.

[1]   Harold Eberle, *The Complete Wineskin,* (Enumclaw, WA, Winepress
       Publishing 1989); p. 144-145.

CHAPTER 3

Expansion
Requires Help

With growing attendance and many calls for ministry, we needed more help. I had been warned by leaders outside of DOVE not to take on too much stress. We were praying for staff to help us. Lucinda Landis became our first full-time secretary and soon many other staff joined our team.

Dave and Beth Neupauer started a house fellowship just north of Lancaster City. Dave had a heart for God and came from the business world. As a business executive, he taught us so much about systems and management. In April 1986, Dave left his job at Warner Lambert, took a big cut in pay, and joined the DOVE staff full-time.

Soon after this, we started the Southern Celebration at Sight and Sound Auditorium with Dave Neupauer serving in leadership. Mervin Charles, Dave, and I worked closely together in leadership and shared responsibilities for ministering Sunday mornings at both the Central Celebration meeting at Abundant Living and at the Southern Celebration near Strasburg.

Youth workers

Donna (Garman) Esbenshade was our first volunteer youth group leader. As the group grew, Brian Sauder was placed on staff as our first youth pastor. Brian had started attending Rhema when he was seventeen years old and continued to be a loyal participant and assisted Jerry Horst in establishing a new Rhema outreach in Lancaster. By this time, he had graduated from university with an engineering degree. For Brian, the switch from an engineering career to youth pastor seemed a natural progression. "You have a call of God on your life," was often prophesied over him and impacted his decision to go into full-time youth ministry.

Brian and a team led the youth group, which grew to include about 150 youth as DOVE started new celebration sites in the area. He also continued to lead the corporate youth ministry and helped train new youth pastors at each site.

In 1991 the first Boot Camp for youth was started with an army theme. The weeklong camp set up cots in the DOVE Westgate auditorium and included worship, teaching, and outreach. Trevor and Jan Yaxley from New Zealand taught at the first Boot Camp, which became an annual event for youth. Eventually it was moved to Fort Indiantown Gap, an actual U.S. Army base, and later to Rosedale Camp in Reading, Pennsylvania. Later, the name was changed from Boot Camp to EMT (Evangelism Missions Training). Many other youth leaders in those early days assisted Brian and Janet Sauder in giving leadership to these important youth events.

A couple from our church who owned a prosperous business gave DOVE a retreat center called God's Mountain north of Scranton, Pennsylvania, near the town of Carbondale. The youth group held its weekend retreats at this center, and we

Our first youth missions camp.

conducted missions training and leadership meetings there. Eventually, we found we did not have the staff available to oversee this retreat center, and it was given back to the couple who gave it to us.

Children's ministry takes root

Ruth Ann Hollinger was our first children's leader from 1983-1986. She and her husband, Lamar, became part of DOVE in 1981 after moving into the area from ministering in Lima, New York. Several adults helped lead the children's worship. Ruth Ann remembers, "Those times were so powerful. There was a sweet move of the Holy Spirit on even the youngest." Each Sunday the children met in their age groups for ten minutes of prayer circle time led by several adult leaders. After opening worship and prayer time, the children split into age groups for a Sunday School lesson. We tried to use small groups on every level, including with the children.

Ruth Ann wrote the curriculum for each class as well as for the cell groups to use to teach children. She testifies that she never felt alone in covering the children's ministry. "I met weekly with Larry, Mervin, and/or Dave at the church office. They were a tremendous support and inspiration."

Numerical growth

Celebration services soon filled the upper level of the barn at Abundant Living. The facilities, although larger, still lacked functional space. Mobile trailers for Sunday children's ministry classrooms were set up. Mothers needed to walk outdoors from the upper level of the barn to the house for the nursery, and children needed to go outdoors in all kinds of weather to reach classrooms in the lower part of the barn. Although trekking through cold and snow could not have been easy for mothers of babies and toddlers, "No one complained," LaVerne remembers. "People seemed happy to make sacrifices to be part of a movement where the tangible evidence of God at work prevailed."

To make more room for adults, children met downstairs for children's ministry during the entire Abundant Living Celebration service. But there was still not enough room for everyone, so a second service was added.

Celebration services birthed an air of expectancy of God moving, together with exuberant thanksgiving for Jesus and His work in our lives. Joyful praise filled the sanctuary as voices mingled with the music of guitars, drums, cymbals, piano, tambourines, and other instruments. We proclaimed the scriptures in Psalms that tell us to enter God's sanctuary with praise, to rejoice, and praise Him with dancing. People responded by standing to worship, and by lifting their hands in submission to the God who filled their hearts with awe. One of the leaders on our team told me one day, "We find it hard to go on vacation. We are concerned we will miss something that God will do during the weekend celebration."

Our updated logo

As wonderful as the weekend celebrations were, we continued to emphasize the "underground church," all God was doing in the cell groups.

Fresh and new

It may be difficult for the younger generation to comprehend, but in those days, few churches had bands or used any musical instruments other than a piano in worship. In fact, at that time, some denominational churches did not even allow pianos. To some, the music at DOVE may have seemed loud, but many wept as they experienced the anointed presence of Jesus. The first worship team was led by Luis Ruiz. In those early days, John Charles played the piano, and numerous members of the worship team played instruments as they sang contemporary praise and worship songs. Many of us danced before the Lord with freedom and joy.

Traditional churches almost exclusively used hymns and a chorister who stood before the congregation to direct them. In fact, I had been a chorister at Hammer Creek Mennonite

Church before DOVE started. But now, we recognized that the purpose of the worship team was to worship the Lord, not merely direct music. Consequently, many of the team worshipped God with eyes closed to better concentrate on praising God for his faithfulness. This was new in those days. The sense of God's presence enveloped the congregation.

More and more people came. The celebration services began to draw spiritually hungry people from established churches. The charismatic movement was sweeping our nation, and thousands of believers who had been in traditional churches were being filled with the Holy Spirit. Newcomers were challenged not to hop from church to church, and to only become part of DOVE if they were certain they were called by God to serve with us. They were told to examine their motives to be sure they were not running from problems. We also encouraged them to go back to the pastors and leaders of the churches they were leaving and thank and affirm the former church leaders for all that they had sowed into their lives.

Newcomers often verbalized the hunger that many Christians in traditional churches were experiencing. One recalled, "DOVE was a breath of fresh air. The Word became alive to us. In our traditional church, we felt lifeless, trapped, categorized. The things we were taught in those beginning years of DOVE are still part of us today. And we still minister using the things we learned then."

Deryl and Mim Hurst, now lead pastors at DOVE Westgate, attended the celebration at Abundant Living in Brickerville in 1984. Deryl recalls, "The teaching was so inspiring and insightful. The worship was powerful." But it was the small group involvement that most impacted their lives. "The teaching and sharing that we experienced in small group (the cell group) was life changing for us and helped us grow tremendously," Deryl explains. "Perhaps even more than the teaching, we were impacted by the sense of community."

But that was not all. "At that time, we experienced a personal tragedy in our family," Deryl recalls. "Without telling anyone, Mim and I withdrew for a few days to a mountain cabin. It never occurred to us that people might want to reach out to us and minister to us in our time of need. When we returned home, numerous messages on our answering machine (this was before cell phones) revealed that people were very concerned for us, asking if they could stop by and pray for us. This experience was an epiphany regarding how small groups functioned and how much these people loved and cared for us."

Commitment in cell groups

DOVE did not have a church membership; however, we did have a yearly commitment to one another in cell groups. We encouraged each person who was part of a cell group in to make a commitment to the others in that small group. This was not a commitment for a lifetime. It was a commitment for the duration of their time in their present cell group.

A card was given to each person in the group listing the points of commitment. At the start of a new cell group or when a new member joined, the entire small group used this card to profess their commitment to each other. This was not seen as a legalism, but as a privilege.

The commitment card stated: I confess Jesus Christ as Lord. I am therefore committed to living in obedience to the Word of God and the Holy Spirit, and to being part of the church that Jesus is building throughout the world. I specifically commit myself to the Body of Christ here at DOVE. I will be accountable to my brothers and sisters in the way I live my Christian life and will support the leadership that God raises up and the vision God gives His Body.

Meeting needs of the fellowship

People were hungry to be part of a church where Jesus was exalted and where they were taught the baptism of the Holy Spirit and moving in the gifts of the Holy Spirit.

At times, leadership felt overwhelmed with all the needs of this growing fellowship, but God continued to give grace to meet the diverse needs. The needs were many. One of the needs was to encourage the many singles who attended services. One time a singles seminar registered 140 singles.

Another new ministry was a single parents ministry called Rebuilders. Steve and Mary Prokopchak also started the Never Alone ministry for single parents. "Many single moms struggle financially, but they don't want to ask for help," Steve explains. To help these parents, "Change-Your-Oil Day," a "Care-for-Property Day" and monthly teaching sessions for divorcees and single parents were offered. While their parents participated in the sessions, children enjoyed the children's ministry with clowns, puppets, and other entertainment.

Ron Myer and Larry Kreider at a DOVE corporate event.

Nelson and Sue Martin began Turning Point Ministries at Melvin and Nancy Landis's farm. This ministry provided housing for youth and young adults who needed temporary housing and a family environment. Marvin Lyons, who has been licensed by DOVE for many years for prison ministry, was one of many who lived at Turning Point for a time.

As DOVE grew, we saw the need to unite people by using a written publication. The *Connection* magazine became a reality during this time. LaVerne and I, along with Karen Ruiz and Sarah Mohler (Sauder), spearheaded this church newspaper which focused on personal testimonies of those involved in our fellowship. DOVE sponsored a writers' conference to equip people to write articles for *Connection* and other publications. For a season we changed the name of this publication to *DOVE Today*, but we later returned to the original name, *Connection*. Today we publish the *Connection* magazine as a global publication once each year.

Corporate celebrations

Because the Abundant Living facilities were not spacious enough to hold the large numbers of people from each of the services and celebration sites, we began to hold corporate celebrations so we could worship together in one service at various other sites. At first, we held corporate celebrations at Landis Valley Motor Inn near Lancaster, where we commissioned various leaders to serve with the ongoing needs in the DOVE family. In January 1985, we had a Sunday afternoon corporate celebration meeting at Warwick High School in Lititz where 620 adults from DOVE small groups gathered. For a season, we held corporate celebrations every four to six weeks at Lancaster Mennonite High School and outdoors at public parks.

Ministering to our children

The thriving church brought an influx of children. DOVE believes children are destined to become the church in the next generation, and we saw the need to appoint Terry Pfautz as our first paid children's pastor. Terry and his wife, Lisa, shared our vision for ministering to children. When Terry became the children's pastor in the mid-1980s, DOVE was meeting at Abundant Living with three services each Sunday. Every six weeks a corporate celebration required staff to pack and set up materials and equipment to minister to about five hundred children from nursery age through sixth grade.

Terry was exceptional with puppet ministry and the kids loved his main puppet, Zap. Terry also wrote Sunday School

DOVE teens praying for each other.

and small group curriculum for teaching children. He saw the need to assist parents in having them teach children biblical concepts. Consequently, he wrote and published a family devotional booklet called *Powerhouse*.

As churches multiplied, Terry helped train and oversee children's ministry teams and even traveled abroad to minister with short-term mission outreaches. A Scotland outreach had 200 kids who responded to receiving Jesus into their lives. Terry recalls, "DOVE leadership recognized the need for excellence in children's ministry and provided whatever was needed. Those were glory years as we saw children respond to God and worship him."

Prayer, evangelism, and discipleship

From the early days our call from God and our vision was prayer, evangelism, and discipleship, so we focused on ways to practically promote these three areas of ministry. People were constantly being trained. Foundation trainings were offered every Friday night and Sunday mornings. We also continued to have evangelism courses taught on a regular basis.

Because we believed it was important for every person to take the twelve-week Biblical Foundation Course, we produced a video series where I taught each of the twelve teachings. After Sunday morning worship those part of the course left the service and drove to the Lititz office to watch the course. Everyone was given a notebook to take notes and to fill in the blanks as they watched the teaching. Then they returned to the Abundant Living site to pick up their children. This happened every week for twelve weeks straight. I do not ever remember anyone complaining about the time of traveling. They were so hungry for God.

The importance of cell churches was constantly emphasized. At times, Sunday corporate celebrations were cancelled. Instead, members met in cell groups. We did this in order to emphasize that "real" church took place in the small group setting. A few volunteers stayed at the celebration sites to tell the new people coming who were unaware of this that we are meeting this month in homes like the early church did in the book of Acts. We gave them places to go to meet in a cell group for that Sunday morning. We prayed in the cell groups for signs and wonders that lifted Jesus higher and believed Him for greater things.

One time, when we came back after a month of meeting in cell groups on Sunday mornings, we rejoiced to find that one hundred more people were attending the celebration meetings.

Rhema dissolved

Eventually, we decided to dissolve Rhema Youth Ministries because our theological understanding in those days was that everything needs to be under the authority of the church, and that para-church ministries were not God's best. In retrospect, I think this was a mistake. We had experienced so much blessing from the Lord by ministering through Rhema and DOVE at the same time. Rhema had kept us outward focused, and I was concerned we could become ingrown.

Because of the concern that we needed to keep reaching out, I, along with a team, started Monday Night Alive the following year at the Lititz Recreation Center. The purpose for this new ministry was to reach more young people for Christ. Every Monday night we taught young people, many who did not have a Christian background, about Jesus. We did all kinds of crazy things such as eat raw eggs, perform in air bands, and anything we could think of to help build rapport with youth and lead them to faith in Christ. We continued to see God change lives at Monday Night Alive. We encouraged participation in the evangelism course and in witnessing at Lititz Springs Park.

Our focus during those days was mainly on what the Lord was doing in Pennsylvania. But the Lord was enlarging our focus to see beyond South Central Pennsylvania. He was calling us to the nations.

CHAPTER 4

Fervency to Spread God's Word

The fervency to spread God's Word to other nations gripped our hearts. Perhaps the most taught scripture among us was the Great Commission: Matthew 28:18-19, "All authority in heaven and on earth has been given to me. Therefore, go and make disciples of all nations, baptizing them in the name of the Father and of the Son and of the Holy Spirit and teaching them to obey everything I have commanded you. And surely I am with you always until the very end of the age."

We also heard from visiting speakers and prophets again and again that Isaiah 54:2-4 was a message from the Lord for the DOVE family. We took this scripture to heart and claimed it as our own: "Enlarge the place of your tent, stretch your tent curtains wide, do not hold back; lengthen your cords, strengthen your stakes. For you will spread out to the right and to the left; your descendants will dispossess nations and settle in their desolate cities. Do not be afraid; you will not be put to shame. Do not fear disgrace; you will not be humiliated. You will forget the shame of your youth and remember no more the reproach of your widowhood."

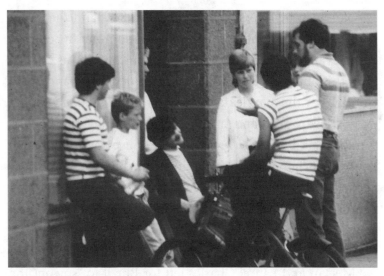

Sharing Jesus' love in Scotland.

International emphasis

In September 1986 we had our first DOVE World Conference with Bob Wiener speaking at Lancaster Mennonite High School in Lancaster, Pennsylvania. For the first time, flags from different nations were represented and this added excitement to our emphasis on reaching the nations for Christ.

Here are a few of the connections we had with various nations in these early days:

Scotland

Our first overseas mission team left for Scotland on August 7, 1983. Jay and Linda Good led the team of 15 young people and Janet Myer (later to be Sauder) was on this team. Jerry Horst and I joined the team for about one week during that time.

Nineteen believers were baptized in Scotland that summer. A year later another team spent the summer in Scotland doing evangelism and discipleship and a church was birthed from this outreach. This new church was led by Jay and Linda Good. Later the mantle of leadership for the Scotland church was passed from Jay and Linda Good to John and Gina Buchan from Scotland. A property with a large house was purchased to house the original church-planting team, but when no longer needed, the property was sold and the money was reinvested in properties for DOVE ministries in other parts of the world.

Brazil

Mervin and Laurel Charles left for Brazil to "spy out the land" in 1985. A year earlier during a time of prayer at the church office, Mervin received a word from God that he would go to Brazil, meet a lawyer and thereafter plant a church. It happened exactly that way through a sequence of God-ordained events.

One of our first teams of young adults doing outreach in Brazil led to a tragedy as a young man drowned and was pulled from the water. As a tragedy usually proceeds a miracle, this team of young adults prayed wholeheartedly and a wonderful miracle followed, with this young man being resurrected back to life!

On November 9, 1987, Mervin and Laurel officially moved to Brazil to start a DOVE church. Many exciting events happened in building the Brazilian church including numerous short-term DOVE mission teams that assisted them. For two years, a lawyer and his wife opened their home where 70 youth gathered for Bible studies taught by Mervin. In June 1992, the

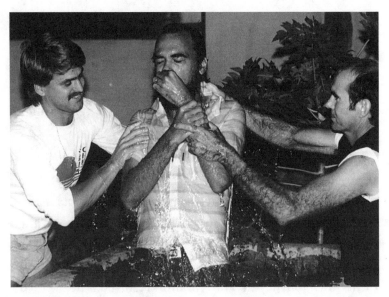

Brian Sauder helping baptize a new Brazilian believer.

Charles family returned to the U.S. and turned the leadership over to Brazilian pastors whom he had trained.

Jordan

In January 1988, we commissioned Bruce and Joyce Heckman to serve as missionaries to Jordan. They served there for many years and later moved to Pennsylvania and Bruce became the DOVE Mission International director for a season.

Kenya

The DOVE Nairobi Kenya church started its first Sunday morning meeting in 1989. Prior to that, Ibrahim and Diane Omondi had started Bible study groups in their home. Remember, Ibrahim was the Goshen College student who visited

DOVE in 1981 because of his interest in small groups. At that time, our hearts had been knit together for our shared passion in sharing Jesus in regions of Africa and China.

Since almost one half of all DOVE churches globally today are in the continent of Africa, I want to take more time to explain how this foundation was built.

Ibrahim grew up in Kenya and was in ministry ten years before coming to the United States for Bible school and later college. Ibrahim was dismayed that some evangelists seemed to brag about the large numbers of people who "raised their hands at evangelistic crusades in Africa," but the evangelists did not see the African believers as individuals, each having his or her own journey in faith. Ibrahim resolved if he ever led a church, he wanted one in which relationships were emphasized. Cell churches, he believed, created an atmosphere of love in which each person would be identified, valued, and cared for.

While a college student, Ibrahim wanted to be a missionary to China. He helped smuggle Bibles into China in 1980 and then went to Goshen College for an English degree that would prepare him to teach English in China. While at Goshen, Ibrahim met fellow student Diane, whom he married in 1983. Diane, formerly from Ohio, had been a math major but after attending the college fellowship church and listening to Ibrahim share his passion for mission, her focus became church ministry. One year after they married, they moved to Nairobi, Kenya, and launched a leadership magazine that promoted Christian values, faithfulness, and transparency.

"We were thinking seriously about church planting, but first

DOVE Africa's leadership seminar in the early 1990's.

we decided to devote three years to establish the magazine," Diane explains. "Writing and publishing the magazine became all-consuming as it grew in readership and popularity. It also became a threat to the Kenyan government because articles exposed government corruption and a rigged election. In anger, the president banned the publication and put our co-editor in prison. The government also confiscated all the equipment."

Dismayed, disillusioned, and discouraged, the Omondis thought of moving back to the U.S. But they also remembered that they had intended to give the magazine three years, then plant a church—and it had been exactly three years from the time the magazine was started until it was shut down. "We recognized God was at work in these events, but it still was painful," Ibrahim remembers. "We realized that closed doors for the magazine meant that God wanted us to enter into another door."

Ibrahim and Diane had bonded with our DOVE vision and desired to see a small group–based church in Kenya as well. But establishing a house church was slow and difficult; it was a new model of doing church and not readily accepted. Diane describes it like this: "We walked around the neighborhood and tried to get to know people, but it was not easy. Most people live life behind large gates or locked doors. Fortunately, our sons who were aged two and three at the time had made friends with children in the neighborhood. That gave me a 'right' to knock on the doors of their parents and introduce myself as 'Mama Michael' (Michael's mom). We invited a few neighbors to a small group Bible study. In 1988, this became the first cell group. We met once a week to study the Bible, pray for each other, and share a cup of tea. We tried diligently to follow up on those who attended by visiting them in their homes. That worked for two or three of the families, but a majority of them found polite ways to become too busy to even entertain our attempts to reach them.

"After several months of meetings, with attendance wavering depending on the week, one of the ladies gave her life to Christ—a significant breakthrough. She immediately became a fervent evangelist. She invited her family members, her friends, and her workmates to the cell group. Before long, our home was too small. We started a second, and then a third cell group, in nearby neighborhoods.

"'Is this a church?' we were often asked in those early days. 'Yes, we have a vision to become a church,' we always answered. We did not want to be later accused of deceiving people or tricking them to be involved in something that was

Members fellowship during a DOVE convention in the early 1990's.

different from what was expected. Some of the early cell group participants were actually members of other churches, so we wanted to let them know our vision. But starting a church was as far as our vision went. We had no idea that God would birth a movement from that slow and rather tentative beginning," Diane says. Today the Omondis oversee more than 200 churches in East Africa alone.

"About one year later, early in 1989, we were asked to take another step. Those who had been attending felt that if we really wanted to be a church, we should start Sunday morning meetings. We did. Twenty-two people attended the first Sunday service in June 1989. We even had a Sunday School class for children and took an offering, which we had never done in the home cell group. After another six months, the office was too small. We started meeting in a nearby school and continued there until 2008 when DOVE acquired property in Nairobi and put up a tent as a place of meeting," Diane says.

John Buchan, from Scotland, and I were blessed to be a part of that first Sunday morning celebration in Nairobi in 1989. We had no idea at that point that thirty years later there would be hundreds of DOVE churches scattered throughout the nations of Africa. The Scripture says it so well, "Never despise the days of small beginnings" (Zechariah 4:10).

How did this growth in Kenya, Uganda, Rwanda, the Democratic Republic of Congo, Tanzania and Mozambique happen? As the church in Nairobi started sending out church planters, many of these people moved on to plant not only one church but to spearhead church planting movements of their own.

"Yes, many times it felt difficult to send out our 'best,'" Ibrahim admits. "But we remembered that God the Father sent His one and only Son. Certainly, we never have a right to complain. Even if we had tried, we could not have planned the amazing growth in DOVE Africa. It was God's doing."

God sovereignly orchestrated what became a church planting movement several different ways. Many of these testimonies are told later in this book.

Ibrahim and Diane readily acknowledge mistakes they made along the way. These are identified as the most obvious:

- Assuming that friends whom we had ministered with and known for many years were the ones with whom we should build the church.
- Assuming that those same friends would recognize Ibra-

him as the spiritual leader of the movement and honor that leadership.

- Sending out church planters too soon, before they had fully been immersed in the DOVE vision, biblical values, and methods.

- Adopting churches or leaders who said the right things but did not understand the vision and mission of DOVE.

- Giving the impression, albeit unintentionally, that DOVE in Africa is funded by and administered from the developed world.

Russia and south central Asia outreaches

In July 1990, Dave Neupauer, Harold Zimmerman and I went to Moscow in Russia to check out possibilities of ministry. Harold, from the DOVE Central Celebration, had started a ministry called Home Fellowship Leaders International and was providing Bible study materials to be used by the underground church. Harold Zimmerman later reached out to and worked with Emmanuel and Jessie in South Central Asia where they now lead a movement of more than 150 churches in the DOVE family. It all started with the relationship Harold had with Emmanuel and Jessie.

Haiti doors open

Tim and Barb Aument from the Central Celebration started a ministry in Haiti in 1998 that would open the doors and connect leaders there with the DOVE International family. Nelson and Sue Martin has been involved in training leaders in the nation of Haiti for many years. (More about this later.)

Sue Martin communicates her love to a Haitian child.

USA Kansas outreach sent out

Our vision to reach the world included planting DOVE churches in other areas of the USA. In the mid-1980s a team of families moved to Wellington, Kansas, to start a church. The team had been invited by a family who were DOVE members from Pennsylvania who had previously moved to Kansas. Within the next few years, some of the team moved back to Pennsylvania. We planned to have a couple we had met in Kansas continue to lead the work there, but it wasn't long until the work of DOVE in Kansas stopped. We were disappointed that the work ended, but we learned so much through this experience that helped us in future church planting.

Guatemala: A school and a church

Julio Rodriguez led a youth ministry in Guatemala, and in 1987 started Getsemaní Education Center, teaching students biblical principles from God's Word and applying them through daily bilingual study. Julio married Jodi Esbenshade, who was part of DOVE's Central Celebration. In the early 1990s, Julio contacted me by phone and asked if he could start a church with our oversight. I told him we would love to, but we did not yet have a structure to do this. We needed more time. Julio and Jodi were patient with us, and years later, after we became a family of partner churches, this was accomplished. The churches in Guatemala are a vital part of the DOVE global family.

Youth With A Mission

Bill Landis, who was involved in the early Rhema ministry, went to YWAM in Texas in the early 1980s to take a Discipleship Training School. Today he leads YWAM in the Caribbean. He helped to open the door for us to develop a relationship with YWAM globally that has spanned many years. Later Ruth Ann Martin (now Bunton), a DOVE missionary, went to YWAM in England. Little did she know that she would marry the Holmsted Manor YWAM base director, Peter Bunton, who later became the USA-based DOVE Mission International director. Peter serves on the DOVE International Apostolic Council.

More global expansion

At our 1990 corporate mission conference, we focused on Scotland, Brazil, and Kenya. This was the same year I met Ephraim Tumusiime from Uganda while I was visiting DOVE in Kenya. We did not know it at the time, but in the years to come, he would play an instrumental part in the growth of churches in his country. More about Ephraim Tumusiime's story will come later. Today more than 140 DOVE churches have been planted in Uganda through the influence and relational networks of Ephraim and his wife, Jova.

In 1992 the first DOVE church was birthed in New Zealand with Murray and Heather McCall giving leadership for a season. (More on our New Zealand connection later in this book.)

Tumultuous year in USA's Body of Christ

In 1987 the body of Christ in the United States faced a tumultuous year when Jim Bakker and Jimmy Swaggart, well-known Christian leaders, had widely publicized moral failures. Churches began to take a closer look at the need for accountability. We saw a need for more biblical instruction, so we began the process of starting DOVE School of the Bible that was affiliated with Buffalo School of the Bible.

Building foundations

Forming a strong foundation for believers became even more a priority for us, so I wrote the Biblical Foundation series to be used for personal devotions and for mentoring others. These foundational studies continue to be a vital part of teaching among DOVE churches globally:

1. *Knowing Jesus Christ as Lord*
2. *The New Way of Living*
3. *New Testament Baptisms*
4. *Building for Eternity*
5. *Living in the Grace of God*
6. *Freedom from the Curse*
7. *Learning to Fellowship with God*

8. *What Is the Church?*
9. *Authority and Accountability*
10. *God's Perspective on Finances*
11. *Called to Minister*
12. *The Great Commission*

Counselor needed

We realized the importance of having someone trained in counseling to teach the counseling course at DOVE School of the Bible. We asked Steve Prokopchak, who was a marriage and family counselor, to teach the course. Steve and Mary had served as missionaries for eight years and had moved to our area when they began attending DOVE. We asked Steve to join our staff as a counselor. For the next 14 years, Steve provided individual counseling to members of DOVE. Although Mary was not employed by DOVE, she shared her husband's passion to see personal lives, marriages, and families made whole through the power of Jesus.

The Prokopchaks put together a wonderful pre and postmarital training course, which later developed into *Called Together* and is now used by churches all over the world. In 2000, Steve's role on the DOVE staff changed when he became part of the DOVE International Apostolic Council. He continues in this position and oversees the work of DOVE in the Caribbean and oversees various DOVE church leaders in the USA. Since then, he and Mary have written additional books to help strengthen marriage and family relationships.

CHAPTER 5

From One to Eight

Our heart was always for unity in the Body of Christ. In October 1986, more than 2,000 people from churches within Lancaster County, Pennsylvania, came together at the Lancaster Mennonite High School gymnasium to worship together as a sign of unity. It was powerful, and over the next few years, this happened various times. Over the years, DOVE churches throughout the world became unified with church leaders in their cities and regions by praying and worshipping together. This continues to this day in various parts of the world.

Celebration sites added

In keeping with our seven-county vision, more celebration sites were planned. We decided to call each meeting location a celebration. We used the term celebration because one of the purposes of this weekly meeting was to celebrate what the Lord was doing in the cell groups during the week. The celebrations were overseen by the corporate DOVE church. Today, this type of church structure is called a multi-site church with various campuses, but that terminology was not being used in the 1980s.

NORTHERN CELEBRATION: January of 1987 was the first official gathering of the Northern Celebration in Lebanon

Ron Myer with leaders from Northern Celebration.

County. Mervin Charles led a team of Ron Myer and Roger Heller for a few months. Before Mervin and his family left to plant a church in Brazil, he transferred leadership of the Northern Celebration to Ron.

Ron and his wife, Bonnie, had visited DOVE for the first time in 1982. Ron recalls, "After attending only one celebration and experiencing the worship and ministry of the Word, we sensed the Lord was calling us to be part of the DOVE family." Soon Ron and Bonnie were assistant cell leaders and then assumed leadership of the cell group when the leaders moved out of state. By the grace of God, the cell group thrived and multiplied into more cell groups planted in Lebanon County while other cell groups were starting in Berks County.

The church on the border of Lebanon and Berks Counties was planted with the purpose of growing and releasing future church plants. Ron said, "While we certainly didn't feel qualified, the church grew, people were saved and discipled. Believers reached out to others and the Kingdom advanced."

CENTRAL CELEBRATION outgrows space: The Central Celebration grew so much that we had to look for a new location and a larger facility. We prayed for a location that was large enough to house all the individual churches for monthly celebrations. To better understand what type of building was needed, some of us flew to see a large church building in Spartanburg, South Carolina, to the Willow Creek Church facility in Chicago, and to a megachurch in Virginia. After these visits, we did not feel a clearance from the Lord to build one large structure for the entire church.

Until a new location was found, we added a Sunday evening celebration. During this season I often preached three times every Sunday: twice in the morning and the third time at 4:30 in the afternoon.

Growth required change

Growth brought exciting but challenging times. Growth required change. In fact, as leaders we often reminded people that change was the only constant at DOVE. People sometimes had trouble adapting to the dizzying pace of change. They no sooner formed friendships within their cell groups, when they were expected to multiply.

We countered this by teaching that leaving tight friendships for the sake of the Gospel was necessary. Although people were willing to sacrifice their desires to reach the world, transition was still difficult. Forming relationships within a new group worked great for some, but others floundered. When three

The Central Celebration meeting site that is now DOVE Westgate Church.

celebration services began each Sunday in the barn at Abundant Living, a strategy was planned to assign sections of cells to attend the same service. Each cell member was expected to attend the same service as the other members in the cell. For some, this was problematic, especially for families who had youth involved in cells that met at different times.

During this era, we made the mistake of asking people to go to cell groups within their own township or region. We formed districts by geography rather than by relationship. In hindsight, we realize this was a big mistake. We learned the church is built by relationships, not by geography.

The small group settings were great for fellowship, building relationships, caring and praying for each other as they focused outward to reach those who needed to know Christ. Cell leaders were taught that they were able ministers of the Word and that God would give wisdom when they were counseling people dealing with personal and family issues. Some of the leaders, although they loved the Word, were not teachers, nor were they equipped to deal with the personal problems some families were facing. Cell leaders were instructed to go to the leaders overseeing them whenever they needed help. Additional training was also provided to assist them in leading a small group.

Serving God with excellence was paramount during this era. Dr. Sandy Kulkin helped us understand biblical personality profiles so that we could work together more effectively. His insights helped us recognize our strengths and weaknesses and understand each other better. DOVE offered these profiles to all those in leadership, including cell group leaders and assistant leaders, to help people work together better.

Within the past few years many DOVE churches stopped using the term "cell group." Some thought cell group sounded like a prison ministry; others feared that people may interpret "cell groups" as having a connection with terrorist cells. Consequently, many churches changed the name from cell group to small group or life group or another term that signifies a small group of believers meeting together. We do not care what terminology is used so long as discipleship is happening.

We trained many of our leaders who worked in the marketplace to be "pastoral assistants" and gave them a ministerial license, which really helped lighten the load of ministry. They were not paid by the church but performed weddings, hospital visitation, counseling, and other ministerial duties.

Input from other ministries

DOVE continued to host many anointed speakers. As

leaders, we attended major events sponsored by growing ministries. A group of us went to a conference in Washington D.C. to hear Dr. Yonggi Cho, the pastor of the world's largest church of 700,000 members. I had taken teams of leaders from DOVE to Korea various times to learn from Dr. Cho and his team. When invited, he agreed to speak at a DOVE Leadership Conference. We used the Lancaster Mennonite High School auditorium and the Sight and Sound auditorium in Strasburg, Pennsylvania, for the pastors gathering and corporate conference meetings. Pastors came from many states to learn from Dr. Cho.

Rick Joyner, also a speaker at the corporate celebration event, gave me a prophetic word about a pruning that would come soon in the leadership of the DOVE family. We certainly did not like to hear those words and dismissed the possibility of that happening, knowing that prophets can "prophesy in part." But later, this prophetic word would serve as a healing balm when the church was deeply pruned.

Prophetic presbytery

During this season a group of our leaders attended a prophetic conference in Portland, Oregon, at Bible Temple pastored by Dick Iverson. This is where we learned about prophetic presbytery, which we continue to incorporate into our annual leadership conferences. *Presbyterion* is the Greek word for "body of ministers." Paul the apostle is recalling a prophetic word given by a prophetic presbytery when he says to Timothy, "Do not neglect your gift, which was given you through prophecy when the body of elders laid their hands on you" (1 Timothy 4:14). The prophetic ministry to Timothy was accompanied by laying on of hands and is an impartation of spiritual gifting. Prophetic presbytery occurs when a time and place is set aside for two or more ministers with a gift of prophecy to bring prophetic insights and encouragement from God to an individual or group of people.

The following month, Juan Carlos Ortiz spoke on stewardship at a corporate celebration in Westgate auditorium. Since we had been reading his book *Disciple* for many years, we clung to every word he spoke. We videotaped him and continued to use his teaching in our cell groups.

Central Celebration relocates

A massive transition happened when the site of the Central Celebration was moved from Abundant Living to the Westgate Shopping Plaza in Ephrata, Pennsylvania. On April 9, 1989, the first gathering at DOVE Westgate was an anointed service. So many people attended we realized we needed to rent more space at the shopping plaza to accompany all the children and that we soon needed to go to two services to handle the crowd.

The following year, in 1990, two Sunday morning services began at Westgate. The Westgate Celebration had grown to more than 1,300 at that time. By October 1990 we were asked to buy the Westgate shopping center. At this point we believed we should continue to rent the auditorium instead of purchasing the whole center.

Originally, DOVE taught that by meeting in homes and rented spaces, money could be saved and more given to sup-

The eldership team of the corporate DOVE Christian Fellowship in the early 1990's.

port missions and needs within the body. However, rental came with many challenges. Rents were liable to increase annually, and a site may not be available on a continuing basis. Some people believed it was more fiscally advantageous to buy a property so that in years to come, the generations would not have costly overhead expenses.

Consequently, the shopping center was purchased by DOVE Westgate in 2005. Today it has been transformed and provides space for Sunday celebrations and many other ministry activities for the church family and community.

Opinions about purchasing spaces versus renting or meeting in homes varied among believers in the DOVE family. We found that what may be the right decision for one group may not be right for another. DOVE churches today independently decide whether God is leading them to purchase a building or not.

A year before the Central Celebration had moved to Westgate, Lester and Sharon Eberly, who had strong pastoral anointings, joined the DOVE staff pastoral team at the Ephrata/ Lititz Celebration (the new name for Central Celebration), which later became known as DOVE Westgate. Nelson and Sue Martin were also on this pastoral team led by LaVerne and me. The Eberlys had begun attending DOVE at Abundant Living four years earlier. Sharon recalls, "Small groups were promoted constantly, and it wasn't long until we were hooked. The home atmosphere and close relationships were awesome. We learned so much from our small group leaders and from the Leadership Training Course."

Soon their cell group multiplied and the Eberlys became leaders. At his job as supermarket manager, people often sought Lester for advice. He was quick to pray and encourage them. His caring spirit resulted in their small group growing rapidly as a multi-age group that quickly multiplied. The pastoral spirit on Lester and Sharon was recognized, and they were asked to serve in leadership on the pastoral team. The Eberlys later agreed to serve as Westgate Celebration pastors until someone else was raised up.

That someone turned out to be Duane and Reyna Britton, who had been serving in Kenya from 1989 to 1991. After they returned to the USA, Duane joined the staff and assisted the Eberlys until January 1995, when he was installed as senior pastor until 2011. Since then, Duane and Reyna continue to serve with DOVE in various arenas.

We have often said, if you understand how a healthy family functions, you can understand how a healthy church should operate. For many years, DOVE Westgate had four generations of leadership who were part of DOVE Westgate Church. This included LaVerne and me, Lester and Sharon Eberly, Duane and Reyna Britton, and the present lead elders/pastors Deryl and Mim Hurst. LaVerne and I feel like great-great-grandparents!

A multi-site church

Even DOVE's larger site at the Westgate shopping plaza did not have room enough to contain the number of people attending all of the celebrations. Consequently, we continued to develop a multi-site church with campuses. The multi-site overseer team at that time included Lester and Sharon Eberly, Ron and Bonnie Myer, Dave and Beth Neupauer, Ken and Judy Weaver, and LaVerne and me.

Although several groups met at different sites, we were still considered one church with one overseer team and one financial system. Each church had a lead pastor and leadership team given spiritual oversight by the corporate church overseers at that time. Those of us in various areas of leadership had a heart for planting churches in the nations. We called this group the Apostolic Team and got together as often as we could to pray and strategize about the future.

Already established were the Westgate Celebration, the Southern Lancaster County Celebration at Sight and Sound Auditorium (which later moved to Lancaster Christian School); and the Lebanon-Berks County Celebration in Neumanstown (formerly called the Northern Celebration), which grew to four hundred adults and children meeting in a rented facility by 1992. Later that year, Larry and Dolly Daughtry and a group of believers were sent out of this celebration to plant a new celebration in Berks County. This celebration later moved to Hamburg and was renamed Northgate DOVE Christian Fellowship. Lebanon-Berks moved to the city of Lebanon and became known as DOVE Lebanon.

Other DOVE celebration sites were started

SCHUYLKILL: The Schuylkill Celebration was started in 1990 by Jay and Linda Good after they had returned from church planting in Scotland. After a few years the Schuylkill site was dissolved, and the people were encouraged to become involved with the Berks County Celebration.

ELIZABETHTOWN: The new Elizabethtown Celebration was the result of a large cell group of eighty-five people led by Steve and Mary Prokopchak that multiplied into four cell groups. The new celebration was sent out of the Central Celebration and Southern Celebration. Mike and Sherry Harder felt called to pastor this celebration. By June 17, 1990, the Elizabethtown Celebration that was sent out had grown to 270 people. Four years later, the Harders moved to England as missionaries and Tom and Nancy Barnett became lead elders/pastors who continue in that role of leadership today, more than twenty-five years later.

ELANCO: In 1992 the Elanco Celebration (Eastern Lancaster County) was commissioned to start under Nelson and Sue Martin's leadership. Even before they had married, Nelson and

Sue Martin were active in reaching out to unchurched youth. They served with Lost but Found in the Welsh Mountains in Eastern Lancaster County. Four years after they married, they began attending DOVE, and quickly became involved in small group ministry. While serving as section leaders overseeing small groups, they also became house parents for Turning Point Ministries.

Three years later, the Martins were expecting twins and consequently could no longer be house parents. Their hearts to provide pastoral care continued as they provided oversight to leaders and gave premarital counseling. Later, Nelson and Sue became part of the initial apostolic council before it became the International Apostolic Council. Nelson has been serving DOVE Haiti leaders for many years and has led DOVE's 24/7 global prayer ministry for over 25 years (more about this later).

Nelson and Sue continued to lead the Elanco church for ten years until they passed leadership to Bob and Trish Snyder who later passed leadership to Craig and Denise Sensenig. The Martins continue to be active in Elanco (now called VibrantChurch), serving as elders. Nelson said, "In my many years with DOVE, my greatest satisfaction is the value that our ministry puts on individuals by recognizing each person's gifting and how it contributes to the Body of Christ. I see this in all levels: small groups, church leaders, and apostolic leaders."

MANHEIM: On January 26, 1992 we commissioned out the new Manheim Celebration from DOVE Westgate with Carl and Doris Good leading this new celebration. About 150 people from the DOVE Westgate Celebration helped establish this church that later moved to Elm and became known as Newport DOVE and later as Newport Church. John and Judy Lentz also led this celebration for a season, and later Allen and Lucinda Dise served in leadership for many years. Several years after Lucinda unexpectantly went to be with the Lord, Allen married Julie and they served in leadership until 2019. Today, Merle and Cheree Shenk serve as the lead elders/pastors of Newport Church.

EPHRATA CHURCH STREET: The Ephrata Church Street Celebration was also sent out of DOVE Westgate and established in 1992 with Walter and Betty Bollinger providing leadership. Later, leadership was transferred to Glenn and Ellen Yoder and the name was changed to Oasis Fellowship. After Glenn went to be with the Lord, Chris and Jenn Leiby assumed the mantle of leadership. Today Oasis Fellowship meets each Sunday at the square in Akron.

DOVE Westgate Church continued to grow even after the three celebrations were sent out in January 1992. In retrospect, we recognize that an enormous amount of change had happened within a few short years: the Central Celebration had moved to its new site at Westgate, and celebration sites had been planted in Southern Lancaster County, Elizabethtown, Manheim, Ephrata Church Street, and Elanco. Growth was amazingly the result of the grace of God, because rumblings among our leadership began about the same time.

CHAPTER 6

Change
and Challenge

Rumblings

Although DOVE taught that both men and women were called to ministry, a discrepancy about the interpretation caused some underlying tensions. The Bible teaches that men and women received the promise in Joel that God would pour out his Spirit on all people, "Your sons and daughters will prophesy, even on my male servants and female servants, in those days I will pour out my Spirit and they will prophesy."

Awareness of this scripture did not always translate into an openness for women to serve in church leadership positions. In that era, a strong resistance to women in leadership prevailed in the church at large. In society, women were sometimes militant in demanding equal leadership with men. Many churches were afraid that women's liberation issues could infiltrate the church.

LaVerne occasionally taught at celebration services and often at smaller events. She and I believe the godly viewpoint of women in ministry is not domination, but that both men and women recognize that through submission to God, they work together as a team. Scriptures affirm that God uses men and women as leaders. When our leadership teams and overseers team discussed this, LaVerne and I thought this conflict of interpretation had been resolved. But it became apparent that it was not.

It also became obvious that some of us in leadership had differing views on how decisions in the church should be made. Some of our leaders believed that leadership should work as a team and everyone needs to be in complete agreement before we make any decision, barring a major crisis. Others had differing views. We had many leadership meetings trying to decide how to make decisions. Instead of finding a solution, the environment became more divisive. We earnestly prayed, had input from other leaders, repented of a spirit of pride, bound controlling spirits, and sought to understand each other's position.

Many of us involved in DOVE leadership were strong, visionary leaders, confident in hearing and pursuing God. God moved amazingly within our fellowship. When the rumbling of discontent infiltrated the ranks, we were confident that God would restore unity. It soon became clear that we needed to address and not "pray away" some of the contentious issues. In addition, some people complained that DOVE was changing; we were told it was not focusing on being a cell-based church any longer but had become a megachurch. They were unhappy with the changes. They did not think it seemed like the family it had felt like in the beginning. Others were critical that people were following a man and not God. Some protested that obtaining a permanent building was not in line with the original vision of cell churches meeting in homes.

Seeking unity

Caught in the crossfire, LaVerne and I tried to establish unity. We sought to listen to those with complaints and find ways to resolve differences. But the fires of dissention could not be appeased. In anguish we begged God to intervene—to bring unity. Instead, conflicting voices, many claiming to be prophetic words from God, came forth. Some prophesied that the whole church needed to be dismantled. Someone had a prophetic word that our leadership was proud. We asked forgiveness for any pride in our lives. We saw the need for restoration and healing among some on both present and past leadership teams and had meetings to discuss this. But with no spiritual fathers or mothers to turn to for mediation, we felt helpless.

Our church had begun with so much excitement. We had poured all our energies into the work as we discussed, thought, and dreamed about our vision to reach the nations. Now, however, it dawned on us that we may have been exalting our vision over Jesus. Although our leadership team continues to believe that having a clear vision is a successful strategy for church growth, we recognize we can never allow vision, no matter how good it is, to take the place of Christ's preeminence.

DOVE was not the only ministry facing turmoil. Other ministries that we had gleaned from were facing similar struggles within their church movements. Some movements were dissolving. Despite distressing news about other ministries going through difficult times and some rumblings among leadership, encouraging things continued happening among us. During that season the DOVE church grew to include more than 2,300 people meeting in 130 cell groups in rural Pennsylvania. We saw this as a miracle and totally because of the grace of God.

In 1991, we could no longer ignore our differences. As leaders, we called our church to seek God for clarity. For a few months, Sunday services at DOVE Westgate consisted of only prayer and worship with no teaching or preaching so we could focus on hearing from God. Looking back, we should have continued ministering the Word of God to God's people, while submitting to the counsel of wise trusted leaders outside of our church to help bring restoration and clarity.

In January 1992, LaVerne and I went to a cabin in the mountains of northern Lancaster County to pray and receive direction from the Lord. The Lord opened our hearts and showed us that we had not given proper stewardship of the mantle He had given us for the "underground church." As we prayed and repented, we felt weights lifted off.

I spoke to leaders about what the Lord was saying to us. Most of the leaders were favorable, but some struggled with the changes taking place. As the senior leader, I felt frustrated, exhausted, and overworked. My immaturity as a leader, lack of training, and my own inability to communicate clearly the things God was showing me led to frustration. In a misguided attempt to please everyone, I listened to dozens of voices who seemed to be giving conflicting advice and direction.

In March 1992, I began to experience burnout and met with DOVE counselor Steve Prokopchak, who suggested that

LaVerne and I take a three-month sabbatical, a Sabbath rest from ministry, to hear God more clearly. During the last few weeks of the sabbatical, I spent some extended time at a cabin in the mountains. One morning I went out for a run, and in a totally unexpected way, I had an encounter with the living God. After I returned to the cabin, I immediately sat behind my word processor (the name used for the early laptops) and typed in what I had experienced. I didn't want to lose it or exaggerate it. I share it here to encourage all those who have at one time lost their vision and need the Lord to gently and lovingly nudge them back on track.

Crossing the creek, no turning back

I had an amazing spiritual experience this morning. I went out for a run, and I took a road that I am totally unfamiliar with. After running for a while through the countryside and then on a winding dirt road that took me through the woods, I came upon a creek (small river) that crossed the road, and my run came to a screeching halt. I was ready to turn around and go back when I heard a still, small voice within me tell me, "Take your shoes off and cross over the creek barefooted." I sensed that I was on holy ground.

I really didn't want to cross. I was not accustomed to going barefooted, and the thought of taking off my shoes and crossing the creek and getting my feet all muddy and perhaps stepping on a sharp stone really wasn't appealing. But I continued to hear a voice deep within my spirit telling me to take off my shoes and cross over. I then began to understand with my spirit that the Lord was asking me to take a step of obedience and faith and cross over the creek barefooted as a sign of humility. The Lord was asking me to cross the creek in faith and in humility, and allow the water to wash away all of the hurts, expectations, fears, insecurities, and ways of doing things from the past so that the Lord could teach me fresh and anew for the future.

I obeyed the prompting of the Holy Spirit and took my shoes off and slowly walked across the "river" to the other side. It was a holy experience. A cleansing from the past took place deep in my spirit.

As I took this step of obedience, I sensed that others who were called to serve with me in leadership would need to do the same thing spiritually—walk across the creek in humility and allow the water of the Holy Spirit to wash them clean of many of the hurts, mindsets, and expectations of the past. The Lord has called us from the wilderness to the promised land of Canaan. We must forget what is behind and press on to what the Lord has for us in the future.

I asked the Lord if this meant that we should change our name as a church (as some in leadership recommended). I sensed God's response: "Your name didn't change when you crossed the creek, so why should the name change?" The change is in the spirit. It would be possible to change the name and nothing would change in the spirit. The Lord's desire, as I understood it, was for us (as a church) to move on from a Moses mentality to a Joshua mentality.

Moses and the people of God walked "in a circle" for forty years. Joshua had a clear mandate from the Lord to go into the Promised Land and take it back from the enemy. Moses majored on maintenance, while Joshua led an army! Each member of the army had clear areas to champion and to conquer; however, they were all committed to walking together to fulfill the purposes of the Lord.

I realized that I was called (along with those who were willing to cross the creek with me) to take the people of God into the Promised Land. In reality, in the same way that Joshua fulfilled the original vision that was given to Moses at the burning bush, I now believed that the Lord was calling me to fulfill the original vision that He gave me years ago when He asked me if I was willing to be involved with the underground church, and again a few years later when the Lord asked me to start something new. I knew I was committed to fulfilling the original vision the Lord gave to me in the late 1970s and in January of 1980.

Barking dogs threaten

I walked for a while barefooted and then sat down to put my shoes and socks back on. As I continued to walk down this road that was totally unknown to me, I had a few other significant experiences. First, the road took me into unknown territory. Less than a half mile up the road I had to walk by a mobile home. There were two dogs barking at me, one on either side of the road. The one closer to the road was a ferocious-looking guard dog. At first, I was fearful, but I knew that I was making the right decision. I just smiled and spoke gently to the barking dog. It hit me as I walked by that there was certainly nothing to fear. Both of these dogs were chained and could bark and make all of the noise that they wanted, but they still could not touch me or harm me in any way.

I believed that signified as I and others took this step of faith and each of us individually in the spirit made a decision to cross the creek, there would be some "barking dogs" (words spoken, perhaps harshly, against us), but it didn't matter; the enemy could not touch us. God knew our hearts, and He would vindicate us.

As I continued to walk, it was as if a whole new world opened before me. The fields were beautiful, and it was a sheer delight to walk along these country roads. I had a clear sense that I was walking in the right direction, but in reality, it was a real step of faith. I had never been on these paths before in my life. I believed that this was clearly symbolic of the future. We would walk in the direction that we believed the Lord wanted us to walk and yet need to totally trust the precious Holy Spirit for direction. I believed there would be a tremendous sense of peace as we trusted the Holy Spirit in this way.

The joy of building

The next thing that happened was extremely significant. I passed an old Methodist church building. A brand-new building was being built on the backside of the same property. There were all kinds of people hustling and bustling around, working together on this project. The roof and the vinyl siding was installed. What was amazing to me was that the workers were women, teens, and men all joyfully working together to fulfill a common purpose—building the new church building. Along with the men, I saw women and a teenage girl with a nail bag tied around their waists. As I absorbed this scene before me, I felt the excitement and the joy and the expectancy within the people. I again sensed the still, small voice within me saying, "This is what it is going to be like as you have crossed the creek, and others cross the creek with you. There shall be much joy."

Just as these people were working together to build a physical building, the Lord was calling together a company of His people to work side by side to build His spiritual building. And in the same way that these workers were inexperienced in the eyes of the world, the Lord showed me that He would use those who appeared to be inexperienced in the eyes of the church to build His spiritual house. These workers were also using new lumber to build this building, and the Lord was going to require us to use new lumber (new Christians) in the building of this spiritual house.

I had a renewed sense that we would experience a working together to fulfill the Lord's purposes that would be much greater than anything that we had ever experienced.

I knew I could not minimize the wonderful things that the Lord had done in past years. But truthfully, whenever we begin to be too nostalgic, we tend to forget the negative things that have happened and only concentrate on the positive. I now believed the Lord had wonderful plans for those who were willing to forget the past and press on to what He had in the future.

And sure enough, the road that I traveled by faith brought me to my destination—the cabin. I will never forget this experience. It was worth taking off for the three-month sabbatical just for this spiritual experience. Thank You, Father, for bringing me to that river to cross!

I now had renewed faith and vitality to press forward in the calling God had given to me—to be involved in co-laboring with the Lord through building the underground church using small groups. I had crossed the river.

Breakthrough

This incident represented a major breakthrough for me and for DOVE. I now realized that I had been seeking significance and security from what I was doing as a church leader rather than from my relationship with the Lord. I learned that "Jesus loves me this I know, for the Bible tells me so." I experienced anew a revelation of my Heavenly Father's love.

I repented for not properly fulfilling the charge God had given me twelve years earlier. He had given me and others the mandate to build the "underground church" by focusing on the formation of new wineskins for the new believers who were being brought into the Kingdom of God, and we had become sidetracked. Nevertheless, the Lord is good. Even though we had wandered from what He had called us to do, He heard our cries for forgiveness, and we received His cleansing and faith to move ahead.

Filled with faith and vitality to press forward in the calling God had given to build an underground church, I shared my experience with our leadership team. To my disappointment, some of the leaders said they could not continue with me and left DOVE for other ministries.

The DOVE family stands together in prayer.

During this time, Mervin Charles had been serving as a missionary in Brazil. The original plan was that when he returned from the mission field, he would become part of the DOVE USA church. However, this changed. After receiving counsel from other leaders in the Body of Christ, Mervin believed it would be best if he and his family moved on from the DOVE family. We are deeply grateful to Mervin for his years of helping us lay a solid foundation for the DOVE International family.

During this season, we were advised by some of the more prophetic voices among us not to use one of the books we had recommended to the DOVE family. Much of the book they referred to included sound biblical teaching, but there was concern about us allowing a spirit of control into the DOVE family through some of the authority teachings in this book. Because we had recommended the book be required reading, we were encouraged to repent for any wrong spirit this book brought into the DOVE family. LaVerne and I went to each of the celebrations to publicly ask forgiveness for allowing this teaching to come into the church. We wanted to be sure we were not overlooking any unbiblical beliefs.

During that season, more people began to leave the DOVE family. Some were influenced by leaders who struggled with our present leadership and the direction we were going. Others sensed it was time to move on.

We saw this as the fulfillment of the prophetic word about pruning in leadership that Rick Joyner had given a few years earlier. Although it was devastating for us as people left the church, we wanted to honor their decisions despite our feelings of personal disappointment. God encouraged us to release people and bless them as they left to help build another part of God's Kingdom. God continues to use many of these gifted believers powerfully in many other parts of the Lord's body. This journey reinforced our call to build the Kingdom of God, not just the DOVE family.

The analogy of a building and a scaffolding helped us understand that people have different purposes in the Body of Christ. When erecting the walls of a building, you need scaffolding to stand on in order to lay bricks correctly. When the brick wall is completed, the scaffolding is no longer needed. In fact, scaffolding must be taken down so it can be used to build a new wall. When you start a ministry, some people are meant to work together short term and some long term. The short-term workers can be compared to the scaffolding and the long-term, the bricks. Both are needed and valued.

The Lord had provided an amazing group of people to work with us during those beginning years. Releasing them was painful to us, but we knew they would be a blessing to the Body of Christ. God has called us to be kingdom people (Matthew 6:33).

Recognizing the need for spiritual fathers and mothers

Although this was a difficult season for many of us, we learned much that was helpful in our ongoing work. We recognized the need for spiritual fathers and mothers as an outside court of appeal. The need for spiritual fathers and mothers is clarified in the Bible. Paul wrote in 1 Corinthians 4:15, "For though you might have ten thousand instructors in Christ, yet you do not have many fathers; for in Christ Jesus I have begotten you through the gospel."

1 Thessalonians 2:7-8, 11-12, 19-20 give a similar exhortation: "Just as a nursing mother cares for her children, so we cared for you. Because we loved you so much, we were delighted to share with you not only the gospel of God but our lives as well. For you know that we dealt with each of you as a father deals with his own children, encouraging, comforting and urging you to live lives worthy of God, who calls you into his kingdom and glory. For what is our hope, our joy, or the crown in which we will glory in the presence of our Lord Jesus when he comes? Is it not you? Indeed, you are our glory and joy."

These scriptures and many others reflect the deep love parents have for children and the need for the same strong parental love to be displayed in the church. Today, leaders and members of the DOVE family around the world have spiritual fathers and mothers to pray for them and help them work through difficult situations. This all came about because of the difficult times we went through in leadership. The leaders we worked with were amazing wonderful people, but none of us completely understood how to make leadership decisions in an appropriate way, and we had no fathers or mothers in the faith to help us.

Biblical leadership

A group of us in various areas of leadership in DOVE had attended a leadership conference at Word Fellowship (now Life Center) in Harrisburg, Pennsylvania. At this conference Ron Myer and I met with Alan Vincent, who explained New Testament leadership and decision-making from Acts 15. We now found a New Testament leadership strategy to make decisions that has helped us tremendously. We explain how this works biblically in our various leadership books and teach the same concept in our leadership schools. The essence of the teaching is that God speaks through a leader, He speaks through a team, and He speaks through His people. We need to acknowledge Him and focus on the strengths of these three principles to make godly decisions that honor the Lord, honor leadership, and honor those whom we serve. This is modeled for us in Acts 15 during the Jerusalem Council.

Despite our many mistakes, the Lord has remained ever faithful. By His grace, we got back on track as a church family and continued working with Him to fulfill His call to experience His underground church. As a leadership team and as a church, the Lord gave us the grace to again walk together in unity to fulfill His purposes. We are so grateful to the Lord for giving us another chance.

During much of this difficult season, Ron Myer and I were the only church overseers. The other overseers had asked to be relieved of those responsibilities. This was a very stressful time for all of us. Ron was an amazing blessing to me during this very difficult time.

After some time, Brian Sauder was asked to join our overseers team. The three of us and our wives stood together through our transition to become a global family of partner churches. On September 10, 1993, we had a church overseers meeting at Brian and Janet Sauder's home. We sensed a major breakthrough when we prophetically stood at the door like a gate, broke any demonic spirit controlling DOVE, and called in the harvest.

Something positive changed in the spirit from that day on. It was amazing! We found fresh courage to be obedient to God. The renewed sense of purpose to focus on God created an atmosphere of expectancy. DOVE's outreach to other nations accelerated.

New vision statement

In early 1993 we sought the Lord for fresh vision and an updated mission statement for DOVE International. It became:

Our vision
To build a relationship with Jesus with one another,
and reach the world from house to house,
city to city
and nation to nation.

Another updated logo

Some years later we changed the word "reach the world" to "transform our world." Our African brothers and sisters added "village to village" to their statement, which is appropriate in their cultural context.

How one becomes a million

The Lord gripped us with His vision to make disciples. We began to teach the simple message of disciple-making that has the potential to revolutionize the world. This challenge is for every believer, not just pastors and missionaries. We are all called to make disciples according to Matthew 28:19-20. I have often challenged believers to ask God for just one reproducing disciple (a person willing to mentor someone else). Just one! If you want to disciple more, go for it as God gives you the grace. But start with one and encourage your "disciple" to disciple someone else next year. It might be someone at work, a family member, an acquaintance from church, a friend, or a person who is lonely. Pray and ask someone to meet with you every few weeks (maybe for coffee or tea) to talk about their walk with Jesus. Pray for them daily!

Every year, the pattern repeats as you each find another person to disciple who is also a reproducing disciple. In ten years, by discipling only one person each year who is also discipling one person, you will have been responsible to disciple directly or indirectly more than one thousand people! You will have joined Jesus' mentoring revolution, which becomes exponential!

After twenty years, mentoring only one new disciple each year, guess how many disciples you will be responsible for? More than one million! That's right—more than one million. Do the math if you do not believe me. After thirty years, the number jumps to more than one billion! No wonder the enemy has been hiding this truth from God's people and keeping us busy in activity—even religious activity. Now for the naysayers and doubters who are saying, "But we do not live in a perfect world. What if it breaks down?" my response is simple: I will take a half million disciples if it breaks down. I would rather see a few faithful disciples than none.

Paul the apostle told Timothy, his spiritual son, "And the things you have heard me say in the presence of many witnesses entrust to reliable people who will also be qualified to teach others" (2 Timothy 2:2).

We have been blessed to be making disciples for more than forty years. We have stumbled many times, but the positive results outweigh the negatives. This is our one-person challenge

DOVE youth studied God's Word together.

to each of you: Ask God to help you find your "Timothy." Take a step of faith and help that person grow in Christ. Mentoring is not hard. You can change the world, one person at a time! Continue the revolution started by Jesus!

CHAPTER 7

Growing Pains

Our zeal to fulfill our vision to expand into the seven counties sometimes resulted in growing pains. For example, a York, Pennsylvania, celebration was started but only lasted a short time. They struggled to find leadership. Later we realized it was probably started prematurely.

The individual cell groups in the Lancaster City area sometimes met on Sunday morning at the YMCA. Some years later, there was a DOVE celebration for a season in Lancaster City led by Joe and Julia Witmer. Later the Lancaster cell groups believed they should disband the former Lancaster Celebration and encourage members to go to other celebrations. This was all a part of our growing process. The Southern Celebration had closed, but Leroy and Nora Weaver and a group from the Southern Celebration planted a new celebration in southern Lancaster County called New Life in Jesus Fellowship. New Life in Jesus Fellowship was later dissolved, but a group from this celebration had started another new DOVE church in nearby Refton called DOVE Rivers of Life Fellowship.

Another big change that happened involved the Brazilian church that had been planted by Mervin and Laurel Charles. When he resigned from leadership, the decision was made for CRISTO VIVE, the Brazilian church plant, to continue to work with Mervin, who later joined the Mennonite Church to serve on the staff of Eastern Mennonite Missions. We believed it was appropriate for CRISTO VIVE to stay connected with Mervin rather than DOVE since Mervin was their spiritual father. Many years later, Mervin helped CRISTO VIVE reconnect with the DOVE family. Deryl Hurst, who serves on the DOVE Latin America Apostolic Team, gives spiritual oversight to the leadership of CRISTO VIVE, but Mervin will always be honored as a spiritual father in that church.

In 1993 John Buchan, the lead pastor of DOVE Christian Fellowship (the DOVE church in Scotland) informed us that he was selling his home in the Alloa, Scotland, area where the church was located. He and his wife, Gena, were moving to Peterhead, where they had grown up. That same year, all the leaders in Scotland had resigned. Only a few people remained. After a few years, this group stopped meeting, which was very sad for us. DOVE Christian Fellowship had been one of the larger Spirit-filled churches in Scotland just a few years earlier. Unknown to us at the time, a new DOVE Scotland church would be started and restored to the DOVE family. More will be written about this later, but I want to emphasize that often what seems a failure, like the end of a dream, is not. Often years later, we can look back and see God at work while we were completely unaware of His plan.

During the years when we had no accountability or oversight, I reached out to my friend Keith Yoder for advice. Keith had founded Teaching the Word Ministries in Leola, Pennsylvania, to serve pastors and help them resolve issues using biblical principles. Keith believed in me when I did not believe in myself. I found his advice helpful. Ron and I began to meet with Keith Yoder, who continues to give us help, input, and sound godly advice as one of our recognized spiritual advisors.

Learning from mistakes

Ironically during this time of uprooting, I began to write more and more about cell groups. Although I felt unqualified because so much seemed to be going wrong, I was told this was exactly why I was qualified. We learn from mistakes as well as victories. In our zeal, we had made some mistakes and yet God protected us, taught us, strengthened us, and

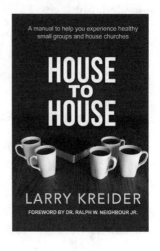

prepared us for ongoing ministry. Eventually, this book became *House to House*, which has been updated and remains an instructional source for establishing new small groups and churches throughout the world.

We often think that we are pleasing God when everything progresses smoothly and numbers increase. But God's criteria for us is to be faithful, not successful. Part of being faithful is trusting God in every circumstance even when we don't understand why God doesn't intervene the way we would like Him to. During our difficult period, we had begged God to give us wisdom and show us a way to rectify the rift so that we could all be reconciled and work together again. LaVerne tells of a time when she continuously petitioned, "God, you must show us the way." God was silent until her soul quieted. Then she heard God clearly say three times: "I am the way."

LaVerne and I realized it was not so much direction that we needed, but Jesus. He is our security. When we seek security in others, we become people pleasers. Godly success is when we seek to please God rather than people. Our desire to be obedient step by step as we walked with Jesus replaced our frenzied pleadings. LaVerne and I learned to walk in God's grace to forgive and receive forgiveness.

Over the next few years, we had times of restoration with many who left the DOVE family. Mutual forgiveness was offered. We prayerfully blessed them and they blessed us. Many former DOVE leaders who are now in other parts of the Body of Christ were so gracious and are dear friends today. This continues to be a humbling experience.

CHAPTER 8

Transition to a Family of Churches

By the end of 1994, we knew we were called to make the change from being one large multi-site church with a few overseas church plants to DOVE International, a global family of churches. At that time, we were one church in many locations, or according to the terminology used today, many campuses.

We felt the vision the Lord had given us—"to build a relationship with Jesus, with one another, and transform our world from house to house, city to city, and nation to nation"—could not be fulfilled under our current church structure.

It became clearer to us that for DOVE Christian Fellowship to accomplish what God had in mind for us, we needed to adjust our church government and be willing to give the church away. Up to this point, all finances were shared with the entire corporate church. During the past few years we had begun using the 50/50 method of finances. All tithes and offerings had gone into a central fund, just like many multi-site churches do today. But we decided to give fifty percent back to the local celebrations to meet the needs of the local celebrations. The other fifty percent of the finances covered the expenses of the corporate church and global expansion. We declared a year of jubilee as the prophets had prophesied. Our overseers team met with all teams and leaders about the financial deficit in some of our celebrations. Some celebrations gave to other celebrations to help each other financially. It was powerful.

The corporate church continued to give fifty percent of tithes back to the local celebration to meet local needs until January of 1996 when we completely decentralized from one church to eight local churches in Pennsylvania.

DOVE family biblical values

We had always taught about empowering and releasing individual believers to their full potential. We knew that the Lord was asking us to release each congregation, giving them the option of joining the DOVE Christian Fellowship International family of churches and ministries or connecting to another part of the Body of Christ. The eight congregations in Pennsylvania and most of the overseas church plants expressed a desire to stay together and partner with the DOVE International family of churches worldwide. As a family of churches, we shared these twelve biblical values:

1. Knowing God the Father through His Son Jesus Christ and living by His Word is the foundation of life.

2. It is essential for every believer to be baptized with the Holy Spirit and be completely dependent on Him.

3. The Great Commission will be completed through prayer, evangelism, discipleship, and church planting.

4. We deeply value the sacred covenant of marriage and the importance of training our children to know Christ.

5. We are committed to spiritual families, spiritual parenting, and intergenerational connections.

6. Spiritual multiplication and reproduction must extend to every sphere of Kingdom life and ministry.

7. Relationships are essential in building God's Kingdom.

8. Every Christian is both a priest and a minister.

9. A servant's heart is necessary for every leader to empower others.

10. Biblical prosperity, generosity, and integrity are essential to Kingdom expansion.

11. The gospel compels us to send missionaries to the unreached and help those least able to meet their own needs.

12. We are called to build the Kingdom together with the entire Body of Christ.

The complete values can be read in Appendix B.

Some trepidation accompanied the major shift from a megachurch to separate governing for each local church. It was a comforting confirmation to us when Glenn Eshelman, the founder of Sight and Sound Theatres, said that God gave him a picture of many DOVE churches scattered across our region, rather than just one church.

Additionally, we found the Lord was blessing the transition process. Finances began to increase in the local celebrations.

Apostolic movement

DOVE International became an apostolic movement—a family of churches with a common focus—with a mandate from God to plant and establish churches throughout the world. Apostolic ministry provides a safe environment for each partnering congregation and ministry to grow and reproduce. This model emphasizes leading by relationship and influence rather than by hands-on management. While a lead elder and team equip believers to do the work of ministry in the local church, the Apostolic Council provides training, oversight, and mentoring to local church leadership and gives clear vision and direction to the entire movement to plant and establish churches throughout the world. With this perspective in place in January 1995, the three of us (Ron, Brian, and I) began to be known as apostolic council members rather than local church overseers.

Our transition as a church required us to form an apostolic council to help us give spiritual oversight to the leadership of all the self-governing congregations. By God's grace, a strong team emerged into a new era for DOVE. Until we were able to add leaders from other parts of the world, a temporary International Apostolic Council was formed: Ron and Bonnie Myer, Brian and Janet Sauder, Nelson and Sue Martin, LaMarr and Naomi Sensenig, Carl and Doris Good, and LaVerne and me. I was commissioned as the international director leading the Apostolic Council called to oversee all the individual churches.

First spiritual advisors

Our first two spiritual advisors were Keith Yoder and Floyd McClung. Later Alan Vincent and Dan Juster served as advisors. Today Keith Yoder and Tony and Marilyn Fitzgerald serve as our recognized spiritual advisors. For the past 25 years our recognized spiritual advisors have served as an outside accountability group, and we draw much wisdom from their years of experience.

This new apostolic team birthed a new category of spiritual parenting in the church: apostolic fathers and mothers. The spiritual fathers and mothers who served on our apostolic council gave spiritual oversight, protection, and served as an outside court of appeal for the senior leaders and leadership teams of local churches in the DOVE family of churches.

Previously we had not used the word "elders" but "overseers." That changed in 1996 with the new church government when we began to use the term "senior elder" for the leader of each church (now "lead elder") and "elders." In many churches, the word "pastor" is used instead of "elder," and "lead pastor" for

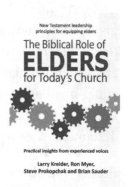

The four authors of the elders book in 2003.

"senior elder." When we study the New Testament church, two basic groups of governmental leaders oversee and serve the churches that meet in homes and gather corporately. Apostles and elders are mentioned in Acts 15:4: "They were received by the church and the apostles and the elders; and they reported all things that God had done with them." This is also seen in Acts 15:2, 6, 22 and Acts 16:4. In Titus 1:5, it is reported that Paul appointed elders in every town.

According to the Scriptures, apostolic leaders are gifted to give spiritual counsel, admonition, and oversight to leadership teams. Elders serve and oversee God's people in an appointed area. Their primary responsibility is to serve, encourage, and equip small group leaders and house church leaders. Today, in many churches, a person who does similar work to a New Testament elder is generally referred to as a pastor.

Process requires time

The transition required each church to operate independently in decision-making and financial management. Because time was required to make changes, a two-year process was implemented to train local churches on how to be self-governed and to have local elders so that we could officially become DOVE International by January 1, 1996.

The importance of involving others and building a team for every ministry, project, and vision became paramount for us. The reason for this concept is taught in Ecclesiastes 4:12 NKJV, "Though one may be overpowered by another, two can withstand him. And a threefold cord is not quickly broken."

We established a stewardship council made up of businesspeople to help us restructure financially and hold us accountable to the budget we set. Today this group is called our Stewardship Team.

Ron Myer led our transition task force. Brian recalls that he interviewed many apostolic leaders to determine the best way to operate an apostolic network. John Kelly, a well-known apostolic leader who led Resurrection Churches and Ministries, gave us insights in forming a family of churches. We visited church ministries and leaders in various parts of the world to learn how to set up the structure for DOVE International. I met with Loren Cunningham and Floyd McClung from YWAM, a global missions movement, and asked them questions about governance for our new movement of churches. Keith Yoder and Floyd McClung helped us with the steps for our transition.

The transition team created a path for one church to become a family of churches.

LaVerne dressed as a bride in combat boots.

We had many transition meetings. We even had a newspaper dedicated to communicating about the transition of changing from one corporate church meeting in many locations to becoming a family of self-governing partner churches who choose to work together as a global spiritual family called DOVE International.

Another major change required was the way we funded missionaries. When we were one church, the missionaries who were leading church plants in other nations were fully supported by our one large church. When we became a family of partner churches worldwide, Ibrahim and Diane Omondi, who were our supported missionaries in Kenya, needed to become self-supporting and raise their own support. This was a huge sacrifice for them and shows their deep commitment to the Lord and to the DOVE family.

Congregational meetings were held in the different churches to discuss the process of change. Our team went to all the celebrations to explain how eldership would work in the partner churches after the transition.

On September 10, 1995, we had the last corporate celebration before becoming partner churches. LaVerne spoke in a wedding dress wearing our daughter Charita's Doc Martin boots. This presented a visual of the bride of Christ (the church) prepared to engage in spiritual warfare—the bride in combat boots. LaVerne and I felt that along with our strong focus on being a spiritual army, we also are called to intimacy with the Lord characterized by being the bride of Christ.

International family birthed

On January 1, 1996, the DOVE International family of churches was birthed as a total of eleven churches in the DOVE family. There were now eight self-governing churches in Pennsylvania, USA, plus one in New Zealand, one in Kenya, and one in Uganda. Each local church had their own leadership team. Our transition from one church to eight in Pennsylvania enabled us to become a network of small group–based churches and house churches partnering together globally.

Each church was committed to give a tithe of the tithes they received to their apostolic oversight team. The lead elders also gave their tithe to the apostolic leadership team. Today, there are more than forty apostolic leadership teams in the DOVE International family of churches and this same principle of tithing is encouraged globally. Our policy is to not tithe to individuals, but to an account given oversight by a team of apostolic leaders. At the next level, each team tithes to the apostolic team that gives them oversight. In many cases, a tithe of the tithe of the tithe of the tithe is designated to the DOVE International Apostolic Team for advancing the Kingdom.

When we became a family of partner churches in 1996, the local churches in Pennsylvania gave hundreds of thousands of dollars over the next few years that was over and above their tithe to the DOVE International team to finance this amazing step of faith that we took together.

Growth during transition period

The transition required much time and effort, but that did not stop many exciting things from happening in the DOVE family during that two-year time period. A business-person from our church gave us free use of billboards placed throughout the Lancaster County area. The message "Come Celebrate Jesus with us" was plastered on billboards all over our region and gave credence to the purpose of our church. This publicity also gave us name recognition. Whenever the billboard company did not have paying customers, they put up DOVE billboards for free.

DOVE Global Leadership & Ministry School begins

In January 1994, Jim and Judy Orred from YWAM Greece spent a few months with us and encouraged us to start our own leadership training school. My response was, "Why would we do that? We made too many mistakes." Jim explained, "That is why you start a training school, so others do not need to make the same mistakes you have made."

The new school focused on church planting and opened September 6, 1994. Brian Sauder implemented the school and has led it for the past 26 years. The first year, the DOVE school followed the YWAM model of two months of classroom teaching and three months of outreach. It was soon determined that it would be more accessible to students to offer the school one night a week and Saturday mornings. For several years the school term was two semesters annually. To enable students to process and put teachings into practice, weeknights were used for teaching, and on Saturdays the students discussed what they had learned as well as received more teaching.

As the years progressed, methods for training have been updated. For example, while Brian served as a school board member of his community for nine years, he became acquainted with different methods of training such as weekend training modules. These were implemented into our school because it was easier for people who worked full-time to participate in a weekend intensive: Friday evening and Saturday during the day for one weekend each month for nine months.

In the beginning years of the school, internet services were unavailable for most people. As it became accessible to the general public, Brian saw this as an effective teaching method for the school. Today, DOVE's online on-demand school is a blessing to many leaders and future leaders throughout the world and people in most countries can access it. The DOVE Global Leadership & Ministry School is set up to function with online classes, notes, and assessments for each class.

"It's a dynamic way to reach remote locations and share DOVE's biblical values," Brian says. "Online on-demand is the trend in education for those under the age of thirty who are inclined to use this method more than classroom learning."

From the beginning until the present, school enrollment has had about fifty percent of students from churches other than DOVE. Of great satisfaction to Brian is seeing the school as a fulfillment of a prophetic word for DOVE given in the early 1990s. The prophecy that "DOVE would become a leadership factory" was not understood at the time. It had been prophesied before the internet had become established. In retrospect, twenty-five years later, we see the prophecy confirmed. DOVE indeed has become a leadership factory. The DOVE school has perpetually trained new leaders and church planters throughout the world. Although the DOVE school is not an accredited seminary training, it teaches core biblical values and how-to guidelines for leadership and church planting.

Teaching through publishing

During the transition years, I continued to write *House to House*. Touch Publications from Houston, Texas, led by Ralph Neighbour, wanted to publish it. At DOVE Westgate each week, I also began to teach a course called Back to the Basics, which included much of what I was writing in *House to House*. The course on the basics of prayer, evangelism, and discipleship focused on DOVE's mission to exalt Jesus Christ as Lord, obey His Word, and encourage and equip each believer in the work of ministry in the following ways.

- **PRAYER:** Through prayer we worship God, bring our needs and the needs of the world to Him, and allow the Holy Spirit to transform us, to empower us and to reveal to us His specific strategies for fulfilling the Great Commission.

- **EVANGELISM:** Through evangelism we make known the glory of God and the name of Christ through verbal proclamation, publishing, the arts, acts of compassion and service to our own neighbors and cities, and also by going to the people of the world through cross-cultural missions. We desire to see children, youth and adults come to a saving knowledge of the Lord Jesus Christ, the unevangelized hear the Good News and churches planted in all nations.

- **DISCIPLESHIP:** Engaging in discipleship, we build relationships with and care for one another, training each other in godliness and good works, so that we become mature disciples engaged in the threefold mission of prayer, evangelism and discipleship. Discipleship thus becomes ongoing, as those who have been trained will in turn train and disciple others. We engage in this mission in humility, with dependence on God, and in cooperation with brothers and sisters in the Body of Christ, working for unity in all that we do.

God uses many different types of churches. We do not have an edge on other churches. At teaching events and in *House to House*, our team and I freely share mistakes we have made and a caution not to become arrogant about the methods we use as the Lord builds His Church among us. Although we have made many mistakes, we are grateful that by the Lord's grace He has taught us so much.

CHAPTER 9

A New Era

The transition of decentralizing into eight congregations was difficult. I had enjoyed being pastor of a church of 2,000 people and the sense of security it brought. I knew how God had been faithful in the past. I knew He promised always to be faithful, but sometimes in the middle of struggle, I did not recognize or sense what God was doing or why.

Throughout the years, we learned to persevere. Not quitting became part of our spiritual warfare. Hebrews 12:2–4 (The Message) poured fresh courage into us: "Keep your eyes on Jesus who both began and finished this race we are in. Study how he did it. Because he never lost sight of where he was headed—that exhilarating finish in and with God—he could put up with anything along the way: cross, shame, whatever. And now He is there, in the place of honor, right alongside God. When you find yourselves flagging in your faith, go over that story again, item by item, that long litany of hostility he plowed through. That will shoot adrenaline into your souls!"

First DOVE International Leadership Conference

As a way for the DOVE family of churches to stay connected and form relationships, the first International Leadership Conference was held at Sandy Cove Conference Center in North East, Maryland. The 1995 gathering prepared us for our transition to become a family of churches. About seventy-five leaders came from various nations.

Today this annual leadership conference continues to be a much-anticipated event. Leaders from every DOVE-affiliated church are encouraged to attend. It is a huge step of faith for many to trust God for the finances to cover their flights and conference costs, but God has been faithful year after year.

Financial expenses for outreaches

The transition to self-governing churches greatly reduced the financial resources for DOVE International leadership to travel to teach and mentor in developing countries. Only a tithe of the tithe from each church was passed on to our International Apostolic Council. Those of us on the international leadership team needed to learn to walk in a new level of faith believing God for needed finances. Later, written into the bylaws of the USA Apostolic Council was the decision for DOVE USA to help DOVE International financially to fulfill its global mission. Over the years, the DOVE USA entity has been a huge financial blessing to our international family.

Steve Prokopchak, who has been on staff since 1987 and became part of the International Apostolic Team in 2000, said that many people think financial resources are plentiful because DOVE has so many churches. In reality, the DOVE International budget does not fully cover expenses that apostolic team leaders need for worldwide outreach. Steve explained, "Many churches in other countries are poor. They cannot afford to pay our travel expenses or honorariums. If a church in Uganda asks us to come present a seminar, we pray about it and ask God to provide. He often does in amazing ways. Provision for financial resources needed to expand the gospel throughout the world continues to require a walk of faith."

Steve, like many other full-time DOVE employees, could earn a higher income through working in secular careers. Steve has a master of humanities degree in psychology and had overseen a foster care program before being employed by DOVE as a marriage and family counselor in 1987. Later as part of the International Apostolic Council, his role includes helping develop healthy leadership teams and counseling leaders worldwide. Steve also oversees churches in the USA and the Caribbean.

Ministry is of prime importance to Steve and his wife, Mary, who served eight years as missionaries before Steve attended graduate school. He said their mission stint was good training for learning to be content with what they have and to trust God for provision. "By the time we joined DOVE," Steve explains, "we knew that Jesus—not DOVE—is our employer. Jesus provides and our increase comes from Him."

For Steve and many other leaders and staff members, serving with DOVE has not been a career move but a calling.

Our call to prayer

Many years ago, we started the DOVE Prayer Watch. Nelson Martin has faithfully given oversight to this vital ministry for many years. The DOVE Prayer Watch is our vision to have people committed to a specific time of prayer so the DOVE family is covered in prayer twenty-four hours a day every day of the week. In it, forty-two people, referred to as prayer generals, are responsible for four hours each week to pray or have committed team members pray during their assigned slot so that the DOVE family is covered in prayer 24/7. This means that more than one hundred prayer warriors are committed to the Prayer Watch. To help the prayer warriors be aware of needs throughout the body, we publish the annual *DOVE International Prayer Journal* comprised of prayer requests. Updated requests are sent by email to prayer generals.

At the time of this writing, more than 90% of all those committed to serving on our 24-hour global prayer watch team are from the continent of Africa. Only eternity will reveal how many spiritual battles were won in the DOVE family around the world because of the obedience of our DOVE 24/7 prayer warriors.

We also encourage DOVE leaders to have a team of personal intercessors to cover them in prayer. We have been so blessed over the years by teams of intercessors who prayed for us and for our family. For many years Shirley Hampton taught intercessors how to pray for leaders, and for a season she led our intercessors team.

CHAPTER 10

Beyond Ourselves: Teaching Others in the Body of Christ

The DOVE family became well-known for cell groups. Doors opened to teach on cell groups at conferences and churches throughout the United States. Earlier, Regent University had asked me to speak about cell groups to doctor of divinity students, who were intrigued with the idea that a former chicken farmer with no college or university degree at that time was teaching them.

At that point, many in DOVE's leadership did not have college education. Our education, or lack of it, was not the reason for the phenomenal growth in DOVE's cell churches. Nor were our exceptional giftings. We equated the source to the same reason mentioned in Acts 4:13: "When they saw the courage of Peter and John and realized that they were unschooled, ordinary men, they were astonished and they took note that these men had been with Jesus."

Continually developing a closeness with God is paramount for leaders and for every believer. Jesus is always the source of blessing. We are not opposed to education. Since then, I along with several apostolic council members have received graduate degrees from various universities.

As DOVE became known for its growth through cell groups, other ministries asked us for input and training in helping establish small groups within their churches. We had so many people contacting us who wanted to learn about starting

Prayer has always been a vital part of the DOVE family.

cell groups, that we decided the best way to handle it was to have a pastors' conference. From 1994 to 1998, we sponsored numerous conferences that attracted leaders from around the United States. Most events were attended by one hundred or more people. Although most of the conferences were in Pennsylvania, we also conducted several in Texas and other states. At one youth leaders' conference in 1997 held in Harrisburg, 150 youth leaders attended, but we had to turn down dozens of youth leaders because we did not have space for them.

Another teaching event, the Cover the Bible series, started in 1998. This took place on Monday, Tuesday and Friday nights, and on Saturday mornings at DOVE Westgate. About 50 ministers in the region participated in helping teach the series that examined every book in the Bible.

Wendall and Ginny Smith from Portland, Oregon, came to DOVE for Wendall's Dragon Slayer Conference, where more than 1,000 people, mostly young people from dozens of youth groups, joined us for this event at Westgate auditorium.

DOVE also benefitted from outreaches from other churches. When Ephrata Community Church used the Westgate facility to host Randy Clark, God used this county outreach to release the supernatural in a fresh way in the broader church in Lancaster County as well as in our DOVE family.

God has blessed us with great relationships with Ephrata Community Church and HarvestNet International, with Petra Church and the Hopewell Network of Churches, with the Worship Center and its many ministries, with Life Center Ministries in Harrisburg, Christ Community Church in Camp Hill and many more. We are one small part of the whole Body of Christ and privileged to serve in the wider church body in God-honoring, supportive relationships.

Orphan churches become partners

At times, established churches request joining the DOVE family of churches. In our early years, we had a clear vision for church planting, but we had not formed a process for established churches to join our family of churches. One day in prayer, I sensed the Lord saying that He has many orphans in His Body. He was calling us to be willing to adopt some of His orphaned churches and leaders if they had the same basic biblical values and vision that we held.

Through the example of YWAM and the encouragement of Keith Yoder, we composed DOVE's twelve basic scriptural values. Consequently, in 1996, we established a path for an orphaned church to become a DOVE partner church and elaborated on the process in our leadership handbook. This process requires a one-year engagement to enable us to know one another better and confirm God's leading. Since then, we have been blessed to labor alongside many churches in many nations where the DOVE family is located. We have not been called to proselytize or recruit churches or leaders, but we do desire to respond to the Lord when He divinely links us in relationship with churches that have no other spiritual oversight and are not part of another church network.

Examples of Orphan Churches

The first orphan church that became a part of the DOVE family was in Sioux Falls, South Dakota, led by Bob and Laurie Brunz. Many followed their example. Over the next few years, many church leaders and churches joined our growing family throughout the USA and the nations of the world. (For a complete list of DOVE churches and current leaders worldwide, visit dcfi.org.)

Another example of an orphan church that became part of DOVE in 1997 is TransformChurch in Reading, Pennsylvania. After returning as missionaries from Peru, Craig and Tracie Nanna believed God wanted them to plant a church in Reading. However, their home church in western Pennsylvania did not have vision to send them as church planters. Craig and Tracie

Craig Nanna helps baptize at a TransForm Church event.

sensed God's calling to plant a cell-based church, but it was difficult to do so without supportive connections.

Craig said, "We saw the clear hand of the Lord helping us in that first year with a divine connection with DOVE International. We were not alone anymore—we now had a spiritual family with the same heart and the same vision for advancing the Kingdom of God through church planting. Through DOVE's oversight and relationship, we met a group of believers in the Reading area who were praying for a church plant in Reading. This small group of believers became a vital part of our new church plant, and some became part of our first leadership team."

Through much prayer, spiritual warfare, and team growth, Reading DOVE Christian Ministry Center was birthed. By the grace of God, this multi-ethnic, vibrant church is transforming

Reading from house to house and consequently changed its name to TransformChurch in Reading.

Today the Nannas play vital roles in DOVE leadership in addition to leading TransformChurch. Craig and Tracie serve on the DOVE International Apostolic Council and oversee the DOVE Latin America Apostolic Team and the leadership of twelve DOVE Peru churches.

Another example of a church that became a partner church with us is the story of Bobby and Wanda Alger, who had planted a church in Winchester, Virginia. Bobby shares, "Before we planted Crossroads Community Church, Wanda and I had attended several cell-based conferences where Larry Kreider was a featured speaker. We connected with his heart and view of ministry, but it wasn't until two years later that we became a partner with DOVE. When we first planted Crossroads, we were aligned with the denomination of the church movement with which we had been involved formerly. We soon realized that our dual connection with the denomination and movement wasn't working. We needed mentorship in a new direction. Wanda and I met with Ron Myer and our hearts attached. With DOVE, we found friends, family, and home."

CHAPTER 11

Season of Growth and Learning

Apostolic Council expands

When the church decentralized, there were eleven DOVE churches globally in four nations. There were eight local churches in south central Pennsylvania: DOVE Westgate, DOVE Lebanon, DOVE Berks, DOVE Elanco, DOVE Manheim, DOVE Elizabethtown, DOVE Church Street Ephrata, and DOVE Solanco. The other three churches were in Kenya, Uganda, and New Zealand.

Over the next few years we continued to grow in Pennsylvania. In July 1999, Al Rainbow was commissioned as the new senior elder at DOVE Lebanon to release Ron Myer to full-time apostolic ministry. DOVE Lebanon is an example of how churches are to grow and multiply, which is exactly what happened after Ron transferred to apostolic leadership. In 2001, about 65 people from DOVE Lebanon helped plant a church in Myerstown called The Fireplace Christian Fellowship, which grew to 200 people with 16 small groups at that time. In 2009, another DOVE church was planted out of The Fireplace in Newmanstown called Living Stones Christian Fellowship.

In my role as international director of DOVE International and president of the DOVE organization, I began to travel extensively overseas to help expand DOVE church planting and encourage those in ministry and leadership. Ron Myer has served as assistant international director of DOVE International and as vice president of the DOVE organization for many years.

In 2005 we had appointed apostolic leaders from DOVE churches in various parts of the world to form a true International Apostolic Council. As we grew worldwide, we started new apostolic council teams in nations and regions to oversee and serve church leaders in areas where DOVE was ministering. The original DOVE International Apostolic Council and the USA Apostolic Council had consisted of the same people for a season. Eventually, Ron Myer began leading the USA Apostolic Council and ultimately there were two separate teams. The USA Apostolic Council continues under Ron's leadership and now oversees church leaders throughout the USA. Presently Steve Prokopchak, Deryl and Mim Hurst, Steve Fricke, and Lee DeMatos serve with Ron on the DOVE USA Apostolic Council. I have the privilege of leading the DOVE International Apostolic Council that oversees the leaders of apostolic teams located throughout the world.

DOVE missions

In 2006 Peter Bunton was appointed director for DOVE Mission International. You may remember Peter was mentioned earlier as leading a YWAM base in England where he met Ruth Ann Martin, who was a DOVE missionary. They

Peter Bunton with a friend from DOVE Myanmar.

married in 1991 and continued YWAM ministry abroad while also helping serve as DOVE contacts for Europe and providing oversight to ministries in Bulgaria, Scotland, and Croatia before moving to the States in 2005.

As the DOVE missions director for DOVE USA, Peter developed short-term mission teams and evangelistic outreaches in the states and abroad. Short-term youth mission outreaches during the summer became part of DOVE's annual Evangelism Missions Training (EMT) events. Long-term mission outreaches were established, and a six-month internship was also started in more recent years.

Medical mission outreaches

In 2007, DOVE Mission International in the USA began to plan in a concerted way to reach some of the poorest of the world by bringing both spiritual hope and practical assistance through medical care. Dr. Scott Jackson, a physician in Pennsylvania and part of DOVE Church Street Ephrata, had served with a medical team in Kenya. He says, "I was in awe of how God used the vehicle of medicine to share the love of Jesus to a Muslim tribe." The tribal chief had told him, "I saw Christ in your people."

As a result, under Dr. Scott's guidance, DOVE Medical Missions formed. Since then numerous teams of doctors, nurses, and pharmacists have treated thousands of people in need. Many times, patients also receive prayer and spiritual counsel. Through the medical mission outreaches, we found that people are open to the Christian gospel even if they come from other religions. Mary Prokopchak, a nurse who has participated in many outreaches, says, "Each trip breaks my heart anew for the 'least of these' and causes me to go and serve again in the name of Jesus."

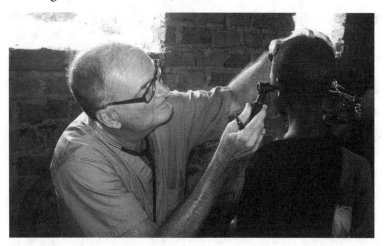

Dr. Scott Jackson, founder of DOVE Medical Misisons.

Missions in Africa, Canada, and beyond

About twenty years ago, DOVE Mission Africa was established to train missionaries from Africa to reach the unreached in East Africa. Led by Diane Omondi, a team established a six-month training course that has prepared many missionaries to go into remote areas of Kenya, Uganda, and Tanzania. Having a viable entry into an Islamic community is a must. To build relationships, DMA missionaries are establishing schools, clinics, vocational training, sports clubs, and small businesses and community development projects.

It has been DOVE's vision to have each nation and/or region develop mission outreaches to other parts of the world. We anticipate seeing dozens of DOVE mission sending centers active throughout the nations. Lynn Ironside oversees DOVE Canada Mission that has missionaries from Canada serving in various ministries based in Canada.

Experiencing the unexpected

While we carry a passion to plant churches globally, not all of them are a part of the DOVE family today. Some have chosen to become part of other networks and some have closed for various reasons. Although it is sometimes met with disappointment or a desire that things had turned out differently, we can honestly say that in every circumstance people were ministered to, Jesus was glorified, and the Kingdom of God advanced. The Lord calls us to be Kingdom people. While we love the DOVE family, we love the Kingdom of God even more. So, if a church becomes a part of another network, or if it has completed its role in the DOVE family for the season it was in, we are excited that lives were impacted, communities were changed, and Jesus was glorified. One thing we know for sure is that in every circumstance seeds were sown, lives were changed, and the last chapter has not yet been written.

A DOVE New Zealand church had started in 1992 with Murray and Heather McCall giving leadership. Over the years, it grew to seven house churches. Most of these leaders were the same age and have since retired without anyone replacing them. Although we continue to have a friendship with them, DOVE no longer has an active church in New Zealand. However, Dave and Alissa Smith from DOVE Elizabethtown in Pennsylvania serve as YWAM missionaries in New Zealand. Steve Prokopchak has led the apostolic team for New Zealand for many years and we are believing God for future church planting in New Zealand with a new generation of leadership.

A Dutch couple went to Croatia to provide leadership to a small group of believers in one of the main cities. During their years there, they poured their hearts and lives into people. When the couple left a number of years later, we knew that lives in that nation were forever impacted by their sacrifice. Before the couple departed, they were able to give the church to a national ministry located in that area.

When we met James and Rachel Krechnyak from Ireland, they had already been successful church planters in their nation. From a modest beginning, they formed a team and grew a church plant to where it was necessary to hold two services in order to accommodate all the people. These were wonderful, challenging, and exciting years of seeing people from various nations who had migrated to Ireland encountering a living God.

Starting micro churches has always been on the hearts of the Krechnyaks, so a few years ago they turned the leadership of the existing church over to a team member and the church became fully connected to the network from which they had received so much support for many years. The Krechnyaks focused their energies on the micro church concept. The first micro church plant focusing on college students lasted a few years until they sensed from the Lord that its purpose had been fulfilled. James and Rachel remain committed to the call the Lord has on their lives as they await next steps in seeing a micro church network established in Ireland.

When a church desires to join the DOVE family, we take time to build relationship and make sure we share biblical values. We enter into a one-year engagement and ask the engaged churches to begin to tithe to their overseeing apostolic team who serve them.

If a church feels they are no longer called to walk together with the DOVE family, we make it easy for them to connect with another part of the Body of Christ that may be a better fit for them. We have simple steps of withdrawal outlined in the *DOVE Leadership Handbook*. We often say we make it hard to get into the DOVE family, and easy to get out. Cults operate the opposite way. They make it easy to join, but try to control people if they want to leave.

Janet Sauder being commissioned as an International Apostolic Council member.

Women's role in church government

For years, we desired to release women to serve alongside men in leadership. But achieving this has been an ongoing process.

Within the DOVE family have been various perspectives on the role of women in church leadership. Some have emphasized 1 Timothy 2:12, where Paul wrote that he does not permit a woman to teach or to have authority over a man as an instruction for all believers. However, others emphasize Paul in other passages commends women for their work in spreading the gospel. Both the Old Testament and the New Testament contain numerous accounts of women who were leaders: Deborah, Miriam, Huldah, Nympha, Chloe, Eudia, and Syntyche. Romans 16 contains the names of women whom Paul commended for their commitment to Jesus and the church. Phoebe was a deacon, Priscilla a coworker, Mary, Tryphena,

Truyphosa, Persis, Rufus' mother, Junia, and many other sisters in the Lord are praised for their diligent work in spreading the gospel. Since biblical times, many great women Bible teachers have spread the gospel among millions of people, both in America and abroad. Both Billy Graham and Bill Bright said they were tremendously influenced by Bible teacher Henrietta Mears (1890-1963).

In the early 1990s, we decided that Scripture allowed for both husbands and wives to be installed as elders, but the husband would be the one ordained. Even though we made that decision at the time, we continued to consider the implications and study the question in more depth. Should a wife also be ordained if she ministers alongside her husband? We decided the answer should be "yes."

In October 1993, our leadership council met to discuss the future of the DOVE churches. This is one of the first times we began to see a fresh openness for women to be included in governmental leadership. We saw this as a breakthrough. At our November 13, 1994 corporate celebration, LaVerne was ordained along with Carl Good, Nelson Martin, Brian Sauder, LeRoy Weaver, and Walter Bollinger.

This world needs as many people as possible—both men and women—who are committed to teaching the truth of God's Word. But as we recognized that people had differing perspectives on the role of women in leadership, DOVE made the decision in 1995 that each local church will make its own final decision on whether to appoint women elders. Some of the DOVE churches had women elders when they were released as partner churches in 1996, and some did not.

In 2011, the International Apostolic Council examined the Scriptures referring to men and women serving together in apostolic leadership. LaVerne and I spoke with each couple on the council to see if any of the women felt called to serve in a governmental leadership role on our leadership council at that time. It became clear to the whole team that Diane Omondi was gifted apostolically and should serve in this way. She is the first woman to become a DOVE International Apostolic Council voting member. In 2018 LaVerne felt called to serve in this way also, and she became a DOVE International Apostolic Council voting member. Subsequently, in 2019, Janet Sauder also became a DOVE International Apostolic Council voting member.

For several years, we continued to pray and discuss the role of women in leadership in the church. We came to the clear conclusion in 2019 that God is releasing women in leadership in the DOVE International family around the globe. I made the public declaration at our International Leadership Conference in March 2019: "'There is no longer Jew or Gentile, slave or free, male and female. For you are all one in Christ Jesus' (Galatians 3:28). The Bible says, 'And it shall come to pass in the last days, says God, That I will pour out of My Spirit on all flesh; Your sons and your daughters shall prophesy...' (Acts 2:17).

"We need women of God to be released in their God-given gifts so men and women can walk together to advance the Kingdom of God. We must fulfill God's original design for men and women to walk together in leadership according to Genesis 1:28, where God blesses them as a couple and commands them to rule over the earth.

"Women of God, we value you and what you carry from God. God's army is made up of both men and women! We are not only talking about women who are married; single women carry so much from the Lord that we unquestionably need."

Then I asked all the women to stand and publicly released them to lead. I asked their forgiveness for anytime they felt put down or held back by men because they were female. I told them, "We need you. We are called to walk together! It is a new day for women in the DOVE global family!"

The first DOVE martyr

Counting the cost of spreading the gospel became a reality in 2012. John (name changed for security issues), who grew up in a DOVE church in Pennsylvania, became the first DOVE martyr. John, 29, was driving to his place of employment in the Arabian Peninsula when two gunmen approached his vehicle on a motorcycle and fired. He was pronounced dead at the scene. A well-known terrorist organization claimed responsibility for the murder and said he was targeted for being "one of the biggest American proselytizers" in that nation. At the time of his death, he was living with his wife and two young children. We honor the courage and powerful witness of this young man who was martyred for the Christ he loved and served.

Examples of planting churches in the USA

Many churches who ask to become part of the DOVE family of churches do so after reading *House to House* and other books on small groups and spiritual mentoring. This was the case for Gary and Bonnie Reiff, who learned a lot of valuable lessons through church planting and saw a need for common vision, common biblical values, and a church leadership that knew their calling and responsibilities. Gary came to Rhema as a young man in the early 1980s, and later married Bonnie and moved to Massachusetts. They started the first DOVE church in the New England area and opened the door for many more churches to be planted and join the DOVE USA family.

In the eighteen years since they planted their first Massachusetts church, they have released that church to others and are planting house churches in New Hampshire. They encourage leaders to share roles and responsibilities. They say, "Our desire is to get everyone involved. Different people host, teach, and share testimonies each week, which allows everyone to get involved."

Every church plant is unique. Building relationships with the community is paramount, but no prescribed formula exists, nor is it an easy task. To give you a glimpse of the ups and downs that church planters face, Doug and Jen Lehman share their experiences of planting a church in Chambersburg, Pennsylvania. Using this example does not mean that it is a better story than those of many other church planters, but space does not permit to include them all.

In his own words, Doug Lehman says, "During the summer of 2004, we began neighborhood picnics in our backyard with the intention of inviting our unchurched neighbors. During these evenings, we ate together, shared a devotional, and prayed for each other. This was no small feat, since the majority of these people did not have a dynamic relationship with Jesus.

"These biweekly gatherings consisted of twenty-five to forty people and continued through early fall. When the weather turned colder, we moved these picnics into a local church building. Big mistake—only about one-third of the people traveled with us, and we lost most of the youth.

"In February 2005, Jen and I purchased a new home that had three apartments. A person who rented one of apartments later joined the leadership of the church. The lady who rented the other apartment went with Jen to a retreat where she met Jesus. By Easter, we began weekly meetings at Network Ministries, located in the heart of the community. Two months later, several young people joined us for Tuesday night prayer gatherings on our front porch to intercede for our city. That summer became known as "The Summer on the Porch." These prayer and worship times quickly became the highlight of our week and lasted two to four hours, sometimes followed by a walk to a local convenience store for a snack after midnight. The Holy Spirit fell, and we met Jesus in powerful and tangible ways during those nights of prayer.

"God began to align hearts, and out of this group of young people came our first leadership team. About 10 years later, many of those on our leadership team left for other ministries,

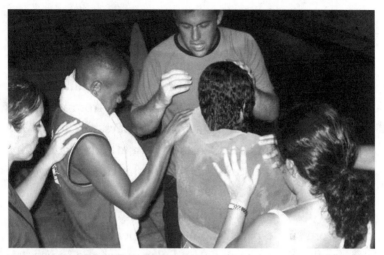

Chad and Chris Miller ministering to youth in Brazil.

and we went through a pruning time. It was difficult to see leaders who had grown and matured with us leave, but God brought other people who have strengthened our church and helped bring it to a place of stability. Our church is not perfect, but it's healthy. For its new meeting place, the church is in the process of renovating an old bar located in a visible area of our town. Fourteen years after our church was founded, we are poised to become what God envisioned from day one: impacting a city that will impact nations."

Example of church planting in other countries

It's often a bit more challenging establishing an outreach in another culture and with another language, but it still requires building relationships. After Chad and Chris Miller participated in a two-week mission trip to Brazil, they sensed a call to move to northeastern Brazil, and after a season of language classes, began teaching the Bible in Portuguese in the city of Fortaleza.

Here is a glimpse into how church planters build relationships with those around them. The Millers remember it well: "We invited a Brazilian team of young adults from YWAM to work with us for ten days. During those days, we showed *The Jesus Film*, held numerous sports events and built relationships with kids and young adults. The relationships built during those ten days became our core group. Within a few weeks, we had fifty to seventy-five kids in our home daily. Most of the youth came from single-parent homes. We opened our doors at 9 a.m. for the kids to hang out and play games and sports. We closed the doors at noon for an hour.

"We began a Sunday evening service and started a small group. We learned that commitment fluctuates greatly when working with first-generation Christians. We had months of solid attendance followed by months of dwindling attendance. In fact, we saw the numbers fluctuating between six and sixty. That is very frustrating, but people need to see you will be there for them. Time builds trust.

"We asked God how we could affect our community and open doors to them. The area was full of drugs and violence. We became proactive, praying in streets, serving at soup kitchens, and bringing people into a safe environment. We saw miracles—including soup multiplying as we prayed because more people than we had expected showed up for a free meal."

Today the church is multi-generational and leadership has been transferred to Victor and Vânia Gomes. The Millers returned to Pennsylvania and served in ministry there for a season. We are grateful for the few years they served on the DOVE International Apostolic Council before moving to California. Today, Chris serves on the DOVE Latin America Apostolic Team and gives apostolic oversight to the DOVE Fortaleza church leaders.

Fulfillment of 1992 vision

In the years since DOVE's inception, we have seen God's transforming work in thousands of individuals who are reaching the world in ways we previously never considered or thought possible. Remember the time I walked on that unknown path through the woods in 1992 and came upon people of all ages happily working together to build a church building? What God spoke to my heart then has become reality:

- Men, women and children of every age joyfully working together to build the church.

- God using many who appeared to be inexperienced and unqualified to build his church.

- Co-laborers working together to build the underground church.

- Walking in obedience and faith, not always knowing how God was working behind the scenes or God guiding our paths but totally trusting the Holy Spirit to lead us.

- Always allowing the Holy Spirit to wash away our hurts, mindsets, negativity, and unmet expectations.

- Committed as an army to go into the Promised Land and take back what the enemy had occupied.

- Ferocious, barking dogs representing the enemy's threats of unbelief, fears, and accusations, but unable to stop God's work among us.

- Having sheer delight to walk along unknown paths but sense God's peace and later discover that God was indeed leading us in the right direction.

People all over the world are doing their part to co-labor with Christ to build the Kingdom of God. They come from many different ethnic and economically diverse backgrounds. They are using the talents and interests that are unique to them to build relationships and grow the Church.

For example, many of us who grew up in conservative churches would not have considered that God could use fashion design to draw people to Him. But that is exactly what God is doing in the Netherlands through Hanneke Develing. She uses her fashion academy to share God's love. Hanneke says, "Some believers wonder why I am doing this as a Christian. They question, 'Isn't it very worldly to focus on outward appearance? Isn't the "inside" what is important?'

"But when I work with a client, I start with questions. Many women open up during these conversations and talk about poor self-image, fear of people or fear of their past. It is then easy to take the step of telling them about God and how He sees us! I often share my story about how I became close to God and pray with them. On the last day of the academy, when they receive certificates, I write a letter to each graduate.

Along with the academic report, I prophesy over them in these letters. I ask God to give me words of life for them. We always end this day with a lot of tears because God is touching them through the words He guided me to write."

Isn't God amazing? Hanneke has her own business, doing what she loves, positioned right where God wants her so she can reach women with the message of God's love.

In contrast, in another part of the world, a man is also reaching others for Christ in a totally different way. Schiler Darelus did not have an easy start to life in a rural mountain village in Haiti. He was 21 years old before he was able to pursue high school education. He was placed in seventh grade but worked hard to graduate in less than four years. During this time, he joined a DOVE church in Haiti and served as a small group leader.

At graduation, Schiler told the pastor, "I want to help my hometown. I want to build a church building, school, and public toilet." All three of these would be a first for his community. Back in his village, Schiler organized a Bible study. He rallied the community to use their horses and donkeys to transport building materials to his remote village. His dream came true when all three buildings were constructed. God is honored as his village thrives!

The two previous examples show how every person in the Body of Christ is valuable and created by God uniquely for a divine purpose. "The human body has many parts, but the many parts make up one whole body. So it is with the body of Christ" (1 Corinthians 12:12).

Just as Hanneke and Schiler may have felt unqualified in the eyes of the world to be able ministers of the gospel, so do thousands of others within the DOVE family who share Christ every day. What a thrill to see how God uses the "unqualified" to build His Church.

Permanent office building

Overhead expenses cannot be overlooked. Office space, equipment, and publishing expenses are part of an ongoing church movement. Our first church office was a rented space in Lititz, but we soon moved our offices to the Twin Pine Auto Sales property near Ephrata, which we rented for many years. In January 2005 we moved from our old office at Twin Pine to the new office at 11 Toll Gate Road in Lititz. During the next ten years we were able to pay off the cost of the property through the generosity of many DOVE family members. The Twin Pine property is now the location of YWAM Lancaster.

Publishing and media communications have grown since our small beginnings and our present offices have been tailor-made for DOVE and its many ministries. We continue to teach and write on topics connected to church leadership and Christian living. Whether through an audio book, free web resource, or livestreamed seminar, we have a heart to share what we have learned with the DOVE family and to the broader Body of Christ.

Many books and materials have been published related to church outreach and ministry. Sarah Sauder has led our publishing ministry for many years. Karen Ruiz served for

Our International Offices, Lititz, PA.

many years as a writing assistant and editor. Hank Rogers served as church administrator and administrator for DOVE International for many years, and Denise Sensenig served as my administrative assistant and more recently as our office manager.

During the past few years, Ron Myer has served as director of operations at 11 Toll Gate Road. In 2020 Jordan Sitler joined our team as a creative director, working alongside Sarah Sauder and our administrative team to help update our global communications and prepare us for our future as a DOVE International family. The practical contributions of these individuals and others on our team continue to provide a foundation for the expansion of the DOVE International vision.

CHAPTER 12

Our 2020 Challenge

From 1996 until 2012, DOVE grew from eleven churches to approximately 200 churches worldwide. Then we came to a growth plateau where we remained stuck for several years. Perhaps we could rest on our laurels: hadn't God done an amazing work? Two hundred churches may have been impressive to some, but we knew that God had so much more for us. So many need to know Jesus, and new believers will need churches—communities of faith. Numbers, we know, are not the ultimate achievement, but seeing lives transformed, living daily for Jesus. Perhaps God was cultivating depth within established believers, but we knew the Lord had so much more.

We could not accept the status quo. Too many studies confirmed what we saw: starting new spiritual families is the most effective way to see people come to faith in Christ. A research study by Fuller Theological Seminary found that if a church is ten or more years old, only one person will be led to Christ for every eighty-five people in the congregation. But if a church is less than three years old, one person is led to Christ for every three members. Read those statistics again. Do you see what I see? We need more churches, new small groups, new ministries to continue to fulfill the Great Commission.

Some people argue, "We do not need more churches in our community. We have enough churches already." But consider this: in many places, younger generations are leaving established churches. They claim to love Jesus but do not sense they are connecting with the local church. We cannot just write them off as being disinterested. At times, that may be the case; however, we cannot simply sit back and do nothing.

We must encourage each generation to start churches and ministries that will connect with their own generation. We are not saying that many young people will not continue to serve in our present local churches. They will and they should. But Jesus made it clear that new wine needs new wineskins (Matthew 9:17) and then both are preserved. The old and the new, serving alongside one another! Every generation needs new churches (new wineskins) to connect with the next generations.

New churches are led by ordinary people with a desire to reach those around them for Christ. These churches continue Jesus' vision to make disciples and fulfill his Great Commission (Matthew 28:19-20).

In response to the Great Commission and the statistics that reveal the effectiveness of new churches reaching others for Christ, the Lord gave me a word from Psalm 2:8: "Ask me and I will give you the nations for your inheritance, the ends of the earth as your possession."

Our DOVE International leadership team felt impressed and believed that if we would trust Him, we would grow as a global church family to more than 1,000 churches by the end of 2020.

Our prayer and 2020 Challenge became 1,000 churches partnering together to exalt Christ in many nations!

We are not disappointed!

We reached our 2020 Challenge one year ahead of our goal! We give praise to God!

- In 2012 there were 200 churches in the DOVE family.
- In 2013 Myanmar and DR Congo joined DOVE.
- In 2014 the DOVE family grew to 250 churches.
- In 2015 we grew to 300 churches.
- In 2016 the DOVE family grew to 362 churches.
- In 2017 the DOVE family grew to 500 churches. Zambia was a new nation who engaged with the DOVE family.
- In 2018, the DOVE family grew to 590 churches. Much of this growth was in south central Asia.
- By the end of 2019, 1,021 churches were either engaged or partnering with the DOVE family. The new churches from various nations who were engaged to DOVE this year included Mozambique, Cuba, and new church networks in Zambia and south central Asia.
- In the new decade we believe the DOVE family will continue to grow around the world. In 2020, a church in Denmark engaged to partner with the DOVE family.

How growth happens

Such phenomenal growth within a few years causes some people to question whether it is genuine. DOVE south central Asia has experienced the largest recent growth among the DOVE family of churches. Doug Lehman, who leads the apostolic team that oversees south central Asia, explains: "We (apostolic leaders) did not plant those churches—the villagers did through relational connections (believers share with their family and friends, who in turn share with their families and friends). DOVE's key is to build organically through relationships, not through structural or institutional methods. This means that I personally do not have a relationship with the thousands of believers in Asia, but each of their overseers do."

The larger a church grows, the less touch each member has with the main leader. Doug said, "It is important for each believer to maintain the same biblical spiritual DNA that DOVE is built upon. The international apostolic leaders work to build strong relationships with the apostolic leaders they oversee, who build strong relationships with those they oversee, who in turn build relationships with those they oversee, etc. Building relationships includes continually teaching core values and biblical truths to leaders, who in turn share these biblical values and teachings with those they are reaching in their villages."

DOVE's growth could even be larger, according to Doug, who said many more requests have come to become partner churches than are implemented. "Building relationships makes churches healthier and stronger in the long run. It takes time to build relationships and transmit the DOVE family biblical values. Paradoxically, it allows quicker growth to happen at the grassroots level."

People often have a preconceived idea that church must be done in a certain way, but DOVE believes that models and structures need to change if we are to reach people. We aren't going to recreate the same church over and over. Each church plant has its own flavor. One may be a house fellowship or a micro church, another a community church, another a megachurch or larger regional church. The important thing is not the structure, but whether discipleship is happening.

Community churches, micro churches and larger regional churches

A community church generally meets in a church building within the community they serve each weekend and in small groups during the week. Most community churches are under 200 people. Micro churches are different from community churches because each small micro church is considered a church of its own with elders in the micro church. Micro churches find it is important to network with other micro churches in order to flourish. Micro churches may meet in homes or other locations, but do not need to own large buildings. They have a vision to start new micro churches. Most megachurches are over 1,000 people and are a regional church, with people driving for many miles to attend meetings. Wise megachurch leaders will provide small groups for people to join for the purpose of experiencing community and mission.

God uses churches of all sizes and people of all ages regardless of where they live or the size of the community. The key is for believers to be flexible and open to God's guidance. Speaking of flexibility, I met one woman who leads a small group that meets at midnight. She ministers to people who work the second shift.

Many ways to experience micro church

LaVerne and I have felt the Lord calling us back to our roots—helping to plant new churches in our own community. Nearly twenty years ago, we worked with a group of young leaders in our county to establish the Lancaster Micro Church Network. So many new believers were discipled during the ten years of this network's existence. When it became clear that there were no persons called to continue on with leadership of the network, we helped micro church members find other churches in our region. But we learned so much during this season of micro church ministry. So, a few years later, along with some team members eager to start a new micro church network, we formed a new network. This micro church network has focused on planting new micro churches, mostly in our community in Lancaster County, Pennsylvania. Here is how it happened.

Brian and Kim Zimmerman from Lititz, Pennsylvania, had started meeting weekly with three to four friends—reading through books of the Bible, talking, praying and changing. More people started attending and coming earlier each week, so they began having weekly meals, then reading and living the Word together. They eventually realized they were actually a church.

At the same time, Chad and Chris Miller were starting a new house church, The Gathering, in Lititz. A group of us formed a new house church network that today is called the House to House Micro Church Network. This network receives oversight from the DOVE USA Apostolic Council and has grown to more than ten micro churches with more new churches on the horizon. The Millers have now moved to California, and leaders from the Gathering house church have been trained and sent out to start two new house churches. The Gathering has now closed. This church fulfilled its purpose in God to reproduce two new churches.

The Zimmermans believe the heart of a house church is relational, and works best with twenty or less people, since most participants prefer smaller, more intimate settings. But there are various models of house church ministry. Some leaders prefer to use the term "micro church" rather than "house church" because these smaller churches do not only meet in homes but in other venues as well.

The micro churches in The Hive, a DOVE micro-church network in Corvallis, Oregon, are a bit larger in size and often rent facilities for their meetings. Tim and Angie Wenger lead The Hive, which includes three micro churches, each with about 30 to 70 people. The churches meet in buildings but prefer to remain small and multiply by starting new micro churches. They meet for a corporate gathering each month, called All Hive. We encourage micro churches of all sizes to also have smaller groups for discipleship.

God has called us as a global family of churches to lead people to Christ and plant churches in the nations. Some of these churches are community churches, some are micro churches, and others are larger regional churches

CHAPTER 13

Vision for Planting Churches Unfolds

Planting churches throughout the world is the vision the Lord has given to the DOVE International family. I remember being on an airplane in the 1980s and flipping through an airline magazine to the pages that displayed all the routes where the airline flew from different hubs scattered throughout the world. The map kindled faith within me as I sensed the Holy Spirit saying that someday DOVE would have hubs sending people out to reach the world.

Today, at the time of this printing, DOVE has hubs that reach twenty-seven nations with more than 1,000 churches and ministries on six continents. Each has an amazing story of how God connected us with key church planters and what is happening in that country today. Space doesn't allow us to elaborate on the details, but here is a listing of the countries where DOVE has established churches and a bit about each one. Some entries include longer accounts than others. It's not that the nations with longer entries are more important than the other nations. Instead, we want to offer readers a sampling of novel ways God connects us for ministry and behind-the-scenes glimpses of the ongoing work involved.

Barbados

In 2000 we met Robert Reed, who desired to plant a church in Barbados. He requested oversight from DOVE and started a small group in his home called The Living Room. Today Steve and Shelly Moore lead the Living Room and Steve serves with Steve Prokopchak on the DOVE Caribbean Apostolic Team. There are three DOVE churches today in Barbados. Early on when I visited Barbados, I met Jonathan from Suriname. Eventually Jonathan started a DOVE church in Suriname for a season.

Brazil

The church in Juazeiro Do Norte is the original church that was planted by DOVE in Brazil in 1987. This church is pastored by Pedro Filho and his wife, Elizete, who have pastored the church since Mervin and Laurel Charles left Brazil in 1992.

This city has grown tremendously in the last thirty years. It is an area with much enslavement to idolatry. A huge statue of a Catholic priest who died in 1934 has been erected on a mountain overlooking the town. About a million people make a pilgrimage to this city each year to pay homage and worship this statue. The DOVE church in Juazeiro is actively involved in helping to set people free from the clutches of this idolatry.

In the 1990s, two more churches were planted in Juazeiro Do Norte, one in the neighboring town of Crato, pastored by Ronaldo. The other in Barbalha is pastored by Bosco.

In the early 2000s, another church was started in the Serra (mountain). Although the people are extremely poor and life

Mary and Steve Prokopchak encourage leaders at the Carribbean leaders gathering held annually.

is hard in this region, the church is thriving. Many people walk miles in the pitch-black darkness to attend the weekly Thursday night service. Recently two other church plants have been started in Caririaçu and Jardin.

As was mentioned earlier, Chad and Chris Miller planted a church in Fortaleza, Brazil, about fifteen years ago. Today it is a multi-generational church and led by Victor and Vânia Gomes. The Gomeses also give apostolic oversight to other church leaders in their city.

Bulgaria

At a cell church conference in Indianapolis, Indiana, about 20 years ago, I met the Tenev family from Bulgaria. They invited me to their country for potential ministry possibilities for the DOVE family. The Tenevs heard about cell churches and became enthusiastic about establishing cell churches in their country. In 2003 they became a part of the DOVE family of churches.

In 2005 the leadership of the church in Sliven was transferred to the Tenevs' son Danail, who serves as senior pastor with his wife, Nora. Danail and Nora also host an online marriage ministry, touching thousands of Bulgarian-speaking people throughout the world. In Sofia, the capital, Plamen and Maya Kolevi and their daughter Liubomira and her husband, Georgi, lead a DOVE church and are starting churches throughout their region by using the Discovery Bible Study method. Many Bulgarian leaders are receiving online training through the DOVE Global Leadership & Ministry School.

Canada

In 1997, two churches in Canada requested that DOVE leaders conduct day-long seminars on cell churches. Through that contact, one of the churches requested becoming part of the DOVE family. Since then six Canadian churches, both community and house churches, are affiliated with DOVE International and overseen by Brian Sauder and the DOVE Canada Apostolic Council. In 2019, Philip and Kerina Omondi and their family moved from Kenya to plant a new church in Toronto. The Omondis had planted churches in south central Asia during their twenty years of living there as students and ministers.

Colombia

Some years ago, Steve Prokopchak received a request from the island of Curaçao near South America to speak at a seminar on cell groups. A gentleman who attended had friends leading a church in Colombia, South America. The gentleman shared the insights he had learned at the seminar and recommended the Colombian couple connect with DOVE. Consequently, the Colombia church requested spiritual oversight from DOVE rather than remaining independent. In 2012, two Colombia churches became DOVE partner churches and DOVE Colombia has now grown to seven partner and engaged churches. Leonel and Alba Vallejo oversee the Colombian church leaders and they are given oversight by Tom Barnett, who serves on the DOVE Latin America Apostolic Team.

Cuba

Outreaches to new nations often begin with a nudging from the Lord to pray for open doors. For seven years, Steve Prokopchak, who serves on the International Apostolic Council,

DOVE believers worship in Cuba.

prayed for a connection to the underground church in Cuba, which is under a Communist regime.

In 2018, he heard that a YWAM Muskoka Canada team with a DOVE leader had just returned from an outreach to Cuba. Through that contact, Steve met Luis Máximo, who leads a network of thirteen house churches in the Santiago de Cuba and Guantanamo City region of southern Cuba. Luis had been asking God for apostolic oversight. He says, "Discovering DOVE at this time is the Holy Spirit."

In 2019, Steve and Tom Barnett (lead elder of DOVE Elizabethtown, Pennsylvania) traveled with Luis to Santiago de Cuba. They found exuberant worship among the Cuban churches that meet in one form or fashion almost nightly. Many people are coming into the Kingdom of God and experiencing visions and growth in faith. The Cuban believers walk in the same biblical values as the DOVE family. Consequently, the 13 Cuban churches are in the engagement process to become part of the DOVE family.

Democratic Republic of Congo

Leaders of DOVE churches in Rwanda have strong family and relational ties in the Democratic Republic of Congo (DRC). Based on these relationships, Congolese pastors often attended seminars and conferences held in DOVE Rwanda. The relationships grew stronger, and a few years ago, Ibrahim Omondi (as the apostolic leader of DOVE Africa) visited churches in the eastern part of DRC. They became an engaged network after that visit and joined the DOVE family as partner churches one

A baptism in Guatemala with Julio and Jodi Rodriguez.

year later. Church planting and Bible training has been a focus of these leaders. As they build through relational networks, and they have seen more than fifty rural congregations planted in the eastern part of DRC.

Guatemala

When we became a church movement in 1996, we remembered Julio and Jodi Rodriguez's request for spiritual oversight as they led a church movement in Guatemala. In 1987, Julio started Getsemaní Education Center in Guatemala, basing its teachings on biblical principles from God's Word and applying them through daily bilingual study. The school started with 110 students and persevered through many difficulties and the country's economic troubles. Since then, more than 18,000 children and youth have benefitted from excellent teaching and biblical counsel offered by the school. The school has received awards numerous years for providing the best education in Guatemala.

The Rodriguezes also started Christian Ministries Light and Life Church and are proclaiming the good news of Jesus Christ. The church is built by believers discipling others who in turn disciple others. Believers are expected to disciple others and go into other communities. Today this church movement is in 12 communities in Guatemala. These Guatemalan churches are a vital part of the DOVE International family of churches and receive spiritual oversight from Duane Britton, who serves on the DOVE Latin America Apostolic Team.

Haiti

In 2008, DOVE missionaries Tim and Barb Aument went to Haiti, a country of high crime and corruption. They worked hard to build houses for the poor, establish schools, and help the people become industrious by starting small businesses.

Graduates of Paradigm Shift business training in Haiti.

Tim started bringing some Haitians to the DOVE International Leadership Conference. Some of them became church planters and now 25 DOVE churches are in Haiti. Many of those churches operate schools in their church buildings because Haiti does not have an adequate public school system.

After nine years, the Auments returned to the U.S., but Tim with apostolic leaders Steve Prokopchak and Nelson Martin continue to travel back and forth several times a year to hold seminars that teach biblical character and business concepts. Nelson and Tim are training native Haitians to start and run businesses to become self-supporting in the country's struggling economy by teaching biblical business principles through a ministry called Paradigm Shift.

Three south central Asian countries

DOVE had its first contact with a nation in south central Asia in 2003. Today that nation is DOVE's fastest growing country for new churches despite its government's antagonism to Christianity and that the area is mostly Hindu and Muslim. We are not mentioning the names of the nations where the DOVE family is growing in south central Asia due to the potential persecution our brothers and sisters in Christ in these nations could face.

Almost 300 churches are affiliated with DOVE South Central Asia. The first one started in 2000 when Philip Omondi and some like-minded university students sensed God calling them to start a multi-cultural church. "We were on fire for Jesus, but we had no mentorship or spiritual protection," Philip says. "I often felt so stressed from carrying the body alone, plus all my studies and carrying on a courtship with my soon-to-be wife, Kerina."

When a friend introduced him to Hesbone Odindo, who leads a DOVE church movement in Kenya with Ibrahim Omondi, DOVE Africa apostolic leader, Philip felt an instant connection. He says, "I felt so connected with them, and I realized I needed a family, a spiritual covering. DOVE's focus on cell churches made it easy for people to connect and our numbers started growing." People representing seventeen nations from many different religions now attend the university church. Since the Omondi family are now planting a new DOVE church in Toronto, Canada, the church in this south central Asian country has been turned over to new leadership.

Networks of DOVE churches led by Sammy and Grace, Prince and Gigi, Emmanuel and Jessie and others are spreading across south central Asia and are led by local apostolic leaders.

Doug Lehman, who gives apostolic oversight to the churches in south central Asia, says, "It is difficult trying to get everyone to work together because of tense relationships among different people groups. Nonetheless, believers throughout the area are hungry for Bible-based teaching and eager to share the gospel with others. They often show *The Jesus Film* in a village and people respond to the message. The problem is that the Hindu religion has many gods, and it is difficult for those in that culture to make the leap that Jesus is the only way to God. Muslims are indoctrinated that Jesus is only a prophet, but many of them are having dreams and visions that are causing them to respond to the gospel. For most, it is a progression that may take a long time as they

Ibrahim and Diane Omondi enjoy time with other leaders at the annual DOVE Africa Leadership Conference.

continue to participate in small group Bible studies. Believers must verbalize to others that they have forsaken all other gods to follow Jesus. In addition, governing authorities in much of the area consider baptism illegal. Consequently, believers pay a huge cost to follow Jesus."

Despite persecution, when they fully commit to Jesus, they eagerly and boldly share their new-found faith with others. Believers in this nation in south central Asia are reaching into neighboring countries that had been closed to the gospel, but now have underground house churches. Again, we cannot name these nations due to potential persecution to the DOVE believers there, but the underground churches receive oversight from members of the DOVE South Central Asia Apostolic Leadership Team.

Kenya

Hesbone and Violet Odindo and the DOVE Kenya Apostolic Council give apostolic oversight to sixty-three churches in Kenya, which includes the regions of Nairobi, Machakos, Kitale, and Kisumu. Hesbone's story is one of many that demonstrates how God's calling to serve Him changes a village, a nation, and beyond.

Hesbone grew up in a poor village in Kenya but was able to study for a degree in India. In 1993, Hesbone visited a Sunday celebration at DOVE Nairobi, where he later met his wife, Violet. Eventually, they started a cell group in their home. Hesbone was appointed an elder and later became an associate pastor under the leadership of Ibrahim and Diane Omondi.

Although busy combining ministry with a career in hospital administration, Hesbone could not forget his village, Kadawa, which was being ravished by disease. More than 40 percent of the villagers had HIV and AIDS. In 2005, a medical doctor had predicted, "If nothing is done, this village will be wiped out within ten years."

"I knew only a holistic ministry could save my people," Hesbone says. "In 2006, I attended the DOVE International Leadership Conference. The theme that year was 'Occupy and Expand.' On the last day of the conference, the Lord instructed me to start a cell group in Kadawa, where I grew up. I started a cell church in my mother's home. Seven months later, 30 people were members and agreed to help start a Sunday service. My wife and I moved to the village to be in full-time ministry. Our departure from Nairobi was not easy because we had

Victory Christian School in Kadawa, Kenya.

bonded so well with our spiritual parents. It was made even harder because we did not receive monetary support from DOVE Nairobi. However, that turned out to be good. It made us dependent on the Lord, who is Jehovah Jireh."

The first service was held in 2007. Today, a service is held in the original church building every Sunday, and ten more congregations have been planted. Hesbone says, "Our network is known as Restoration Community Church. The Lord is delivering many from darkness, immorality, drug addiction, and witchcraft. As people are taught hygiene, it has helped stop cholera. HIV/AIDS and other infections are declining due to changes in behavior. Malaria cases have been reduced through mosquito bed net distributions and by removing bushes around houses. The latest demographic shows life expectancy has improved from 37–40 years to 45–60 years. Ignorance is being reduced as parents enroll their children in school. Many orphans are attending boarding school due to divine partnerships. Destitute widows are being cared for; wetlands that were not producing food are now productive farms. In addition, neighboring churches are being transformed as they hear and are challenged by what God is doing. The transformation of Kadawa would not have happened without the prayer and financial resources of the DOVE family and other divine partnerships."

Hesbone and Violet Odindo joined the DOVE International Apostolic Council Team in March 2014 and have been a great blessing to the DOVE International family.

Many additional churches have been planted in other regions of Kenya. These regions are led by local apostolic leaders, and lead elders and their teams lead the local churches. This includes churches in Machakos County, the Kitale region, and the Nairobi region. There are so many stories of God's grace and blessing in Kenya as churches have been planted throughout the nation.

Mozambique

DOVE in Mozambique is led by Jose and Camila Hernandez, young pastors with a burning desire to see their nation transformed for Christ. Both Jose and Camila studied in Asia, where they met Philip and Kerina Omondi through a common friend. After they finished studying at the university, they rejected several job offers in order to return to Mozambique and pursue their passion for church planting. Two churches in Mozambique are engaged with the DOVE International family and look forward to becoming partner churches soon.

DOVE leaders representing Mozambique, Zambia and Kenya.

Myanmar

DOVE Myanmar was established in 2015 and now has 79 churches, many of which are house churches. Ram Khaw Lian, who leads DOVE Myanmar, heard about house church networks in 2005 after reading our book *House Church Networks.* Immediately Ram desired to connect with DOVE International because its vision, biblical values, and statement of faith duplicated his own. But it wasn't until 2015 that the Lord opened the way for him to meet with me when I spoke at a conference in Bangkok, Thailand.

Ram says, "I was longing for an international spiritual family connection in my heart." Before that, Ram, his wife, Novel, and two daughters had started the Grace Family Christian Network (GFCN), which grew into a network of house churches. God touched the hearts of Ram and fellow Chris-

DOVE believers in Myanmar.

tians when they saw that many orphans and poor children were sent to Buddhist monasteries. In response to the need, the church opened orphanages for abandoned children and orphans. They also opened a Christian institute that now has more than 300 alumni serving the Lord.

Christians in Myanmar face increased persecution such as detentions, abduction, and the invasion of church properties. Religious nationalism, fueled by the majority religion of their country, is instigating an increase in the fight against ethnic and religious minorities, which includes Christians.

"Living by faith is very hard, especially in poor countries. But the joy of our spirits is incomparable to anything else in the world when God gives us victory in the ministry," Ram says.

The Netherlands and Denmark

Dirk and Hanneke Develing lead The Living in the Netherlands, founded in 2008. Unique ways to reach young people were demonstrated by this Dutch outreach which incorporated disco music with worship and teaching. Like many youth outreaches, this is an evolving ministry. The youth grew up, established careers, married, and many moved out of the area. However, the same leaders remained and rebooted their outreach to mentoring, house church ministering, and releasing others to start ministries. The Develings also oversee a new DOVE engaged church in Denmark.

In 2019 Dirk and Hanneke were affirmed to join the DOVE Europe Apostolic Team, presently led by Ron Myer. Peter Bunton and I also serve on this team. We have urgently wanted to see Europeans on this team for many years, so we are very grateful. This team oversees Scotland, Bulgaria, Denmark, and the Netherlands.

Peru

DOVE pastors Craig and Tracie Nanna had been missionaries to Peru before they began DOVE Reading (now TransformChurch). They continued traveling back and forth to Peru yearly to encourage the church there. When the oversight of the Peru network of churches disbanded, Justo and Loren Llecllish asked for oversight and connection with DOVE in 2002.

Lima, the city where they minister, is growing so rapidly that traveling for a celebration meeting sometimes requires

Justo and Loren Llecllish lead micro churches throughout Lima, Peru.

three hours to get from one side of the city to the other. Consequently, the church, Héroes 21, decided to establish small micro churches in various districts of Lima. Small groups were formed for university students, business people, and families to meet in coffee shops, restaurants, and homes in the areas where they live. The simple strategy of not needing a building but meeting as a church family has grown to include twelve micro churches. Several of these micro churches have contacts with believers in Spain, Argentina, and other countries where the idea of simple church—no building but believers gathering for worship and Bible study—are causing them to meet as church families.

Philippines

Thirty-one churches have joined DOVE Philippines since it was birthed in 2011. Jeff and Tonya Hoglen, leaders of the DOVE Philippines Apostolic Team, were instrumental in working with many leaders to plant many of these churches. Some of them were planted by graduates of the DOVE Leadership and Ministry School in the Philippines, which consists of live classrooms, DVDs for distance learning, and accelerated seminar formations. They also write discipleship booklets for the Filipino context. A DOVE youth movement in the Philippines is reaching over a thousand young people throughout Luzon through camps, concerts, and sports.

Unique sites are used as church facilities in the Philippines. Many of the churches start as a Bible study and morph into

Worshipping the Lord in the Philippines.

a Sunday gathering that meets in places such as restaurants, coffee shops and classrooms. This method allows for church planting on a "shoestring" budget.

In rural areas, the idea of house church is not only accepted but embraced. The worship service of one new church in Rizal is held in a carport area. The catalyst was simply willing church members who opened their home and grounds after the church began a feeding program for children and soccer clinics for teens.

The churches in the Philippines are active within the local police departments, military, and local government. Pastors lead morning devotions in all these areas of government. DOVE Philippines is active in all three areas of the Philippines–Luzon, the Visayas and Mindanao.

Rwanda

The nations of East Africa share many things in common. Based on mutual friendships and Kingdom connections, Ephraim Tumusiime, Uganda's apostolic leader, met Levis Kagigi, a Rwandan church leader. Levis attended seminars held in DOVE Uganda, and the relationship was strengthened. In May 2003, Levis's church in Kigali entered an engagement period with DOVE. Two years later, they became a partner church in the DOVE International family. Since then, nine other churches have been planted.

Things became extremely difficult in Rwanda when the president closed more than 6,000 churches nationwide. Seven out of the ten DOVE churches in Rwanda had to stop all services. Lack of amenities such as parking lots, sound proofing and adequate restroom facilities were cited for these closures. DOVE churches went underground for a season. In 2019, the main church in the capital city, Kanombe, reopened after fulfilling government requirements.

Rwanda has suffered immensely from civil war, tribal clashes, and genocide. The Rwandan government emphasizes there is only one people group in Rwanda—no tribes or factions. This sounds fine on the surface, but it does not reflect the reality of the deep wounds most people carry. Hatred and revenge can be tangibly felt today.

The Congolese are not left out of the dilemma, since the region of Bukavu where DOVE churches are based was home to Rwandan refugees who ravaged the land two generations ago. In June 2017, DOVE leaders from Uganda and Kenya came together with churches from Rwanda and DR Congo to support this healing process. Testimonies of those who have allowed God to bandage their wounds display the greatest impact.

One such testimony by Jared (not his real name) explained that after his father and uncle were killed in the Rwanda genocide of 1994, he joined a gang of young men from his tribe. They planned how they would take revenge on the killers. Soon after Jared received Christ and things changed for him, he abandoned his plans to get even and forgave instead.

When the people who killed Jared's father were released, he extended forgiveness—even though his mother and sister thought he had lost his mind. As was the case with Jared, many Rwandans are dealing afresh with trauma as people who were imprisoned after the genocide are now being released.

These people are once again walking the streets and causing a response of fear and unrest.

Participants in the gathering went through an intentional process: one tribe confessing the atrocities they carried out; one tribe repenting for the hatred they harbored; Rwandans asking forgiveness from the Congolese, whose land they plundered. Forgiveness was extended in every case. This acknowledgement of wrong and extension of forgiveness was a great source of relief and healing. Clearly God is at work not only to heal but to extend His Kingdom in this region of Africa.

Scotland

In 2001 and 2002, two churches in northern Scotland joined the DOVE International family. This was exciting for us because it was disappointing when the church in central Scotland had decided to leave DOVE in 1996. One new church plant was started in Peterhead, Scotland, by a Scottish couple who had come to Pennsylvania to take our leadership school. They were in the DOVE family for a season, but later felt called to move on to connect with other leaders in the United Kingdom.

By this time, John Buchan and his wife, Gena, who had been leading the original DOVE Scotland church before they moved to Peterhead, established a new DOVE church, Living Waters Community Church, and led it until John's death in 2015. Today the DOVE church in Peterhead is led by Nick and Liz Wilson, whom we met in Scotland when we sent our first mission team there 35 years earlier. In 2019, five interns from DOVE churches in the USA went to Peterhead for six months

Merle and Cheree Shenk with Ralph and Valerie Klein from Cape Town, South Africa.

to help the church establish a youth outreach. The Scotland church has a heart to reach the next generation for Christ.

South Africa

Merle and Cheree Shenk planted House of Praise in inner-city Cape Town in 2005. God led them to connect with DOVE International in 2008. Since then, DOVE South Africa has grown to four churches in this culturally diverse nation that is historically known for racial division.

When the Shenks first moved to South Africa, God opened a door for them to lead a small group in Cape Town's inner city called Woodstock, which is one of the most dangerous regions in the province due to gangs and drugs. "We saw the hand of God as we did street evangelism and one-on-one discipleship," Merle says.

They experienced an incredible environment where God was healing, people were ministering prophetically to each other, and many people were giving their lives to Jesus. Bodies were brought to wholeness from cancer, HIV, sepsis, and other various infections and ailments. Financial miracles and supernatural manifestation on the streets overflowed from what the Lord was regularly doing in church services.

Merle and Cheree Shenk sensed God calling them back to the USA, where they now pastor Newport Church in Pennsylvania and serve on the DOVE International Apostolic Council Team.

Merle says, "We handed over the lead pastor role to Nigel and Samantha Okkers, who had been part of our leadership teams for seven years."

Tanzania

Mark and Rachael Gotts, British and Kenyan respectively, felt a strong call to Tanzania after learning about house churches and house church movements through DOVE's teachings. They linked up with DOVE Africa and were sent as church planters to Tanzania. After almost two years of prayer on-site with very little visible fruit, the Gotts are now in the center of revival. In just three months, 17 house churches have sprung up, almost half of these comprised of Muslim-background believers. Jesus is appearing to Muslims in Tanzania. After an encounter with Jesus, they seek out Christians who can teach them in the way of Christ. Some are meeting in caves or other

Children in worship in Uganda.

secret locations, but the Word of God is going forth with signs and wonders following.

Uganda

In the late 1980s, Ibrahim Omondi and I and a small team walked across the border of Kenya into Uganda and asked the Lord for new believers and new churches in Uganda. A few years later, Ephraim Tumusiime from Uganda became a member of DOVE while studying for his master's degree in communication in Nairobi, Kenya. A few years earlier, Ephraim was disillusioned and abandoned by a North American missionary with whom he had worked side by side. Together, they had planted about four hundred churches in Uganda. He had looked to this man as a spiritual father, but the relationship began to unravel when Ephraim noticed that money was the bottom line for the missionary. It turned out that the missionary cared less about the souls brought to the Lord through church planting and more about financial gain.

Ephraim felt taken advantage of by someone he had trusted much. Ephraim attempted to untangle himself from the North American missionary's web of deception and greed, narrowly escaping harm when the missionary sent thugs to burn down Ephraim's house. Shell-shocked and grieving, reluctant to ever trust again, Ephraim moved to the neighboring nation of Kenya and enrolled in a university. He heard about DOVE from students at the university and started attending.

Ephraim explains, "The warmth I felt in DOVE Nairobi through the relationships I developed with members encouraged me to participate in the whole life of the church. I particularly became excited by the relationships built in the church through cell groups."

When in Nairobi, Ephraim had no interest in going back to church work. But at the same time, he longed to see the depth of fellowship he experienced in the DOVE cell groups replicated in his country. Ibrahim encouraged him to pray about starting DOVE in Uganda. Despite many misgivings, he did.

"When I moved back to Kampala, Uganda, my wife, Jova, and I started a new church in our home," Ephraim says. "We met on our porch and hung up a tarp to keep us dry when it rained. I learned that I should pray that the Lord would bring people who would become part of the outreach. The Lord indeed brought people, many of whom I had never met.

"It is exciting to see the lost getting found and becoming believers," Ephraim testifies. "It is within the fellowship that new believers are discipled. As they are transformed into Christ-likeness and serve, the joy of ministry becomes unequalled as we see the recent enemies of the cross defending it! That is why I like starting churches—and have planted more than one hundred churches.

"A few years ago, exciting work began among South Sudanese refugees in northern Uganda. A typical example of how we begin a new church can be seen in how we planted a church at Rhino Camp Refugee Settlement in Arua District. Live music, dancing, and the sound of a ram's horn enticed refugees to gather from different parts of the refugee camp to hear the Word of the Lord. A young refugee from the Congo preached powerfully in English. Because the majority of the refugees are from South Sudan, the message was interpreted into Arabic. During the altar call, more than eighty people gave their lives to Christ!

"DOVE Uganda has also started four early childhood development centers [ECDC] within the four refugee clusters of Rhino Camp. The four clusters house more than 15,000 refugees. Each ECDC has about 250 hungry children. The refugees are very needy and it requires a lot of funds to pay teachers, provide meals for children, and comply with the government's requirement for us to provide pit latrines, playgrounds with play materials, and proper structure for learning with seats and fenced learning areas.

"We are building Kingdom relationships with the refugees. When peace returns to northeastern Democratic Republic of the Congo and the Republic of South Sudan, the refugees will return home, and DOVE will have bases from which Bible-believing congregations will be planted. Such church planting vision excites me. That's why I love planting churches!"

DOVE Colombian believers help Venezuelan brothers and sisters.

Venezuela

News reports do not adequately portray the anxiety and pain most Venezuelans are going through from its government upheaval. The country suffers from a lack of food and medicine.

In 2018, a team led by Juan Pablo Muñoz and his wife, Adriana, who serve as lead elders of a DOVE church in Colombia, traveled to Venezuela to share God's love and set up soup kitchens to feed almost seven hundred people and help make repairs to a church building.

Through ongoing relationships with DOVE Colombia, two Venezuelan churches are engaged to partner with the DOVE family. Monies raised by DOVE leaders at a leadership conference enabled the Venezuelan churches to start agriculture projects that provide food for the community. The agricultural work has also enabled the church to provide housing and care for many orphan teenagers who help with the work. DOVE Venezuela overseers Federico and Orneida Himiol have attained government permits for the churches to become community centers. Juan Pablo and Adriana Muñoz from Colombia serve in apostolic oversight for the DOVE Venezuela overseers.

Zambia

In the early 2000s, Ibrahim Omondi and I visited Zambia and prayed for new churches to be planted there through the DOVE family. DOVE Zambia started a few years ago after an existing church network reached out to DOVE International seeking connection and partnership. Dan and Regina Bumstead were serving as DMI missionaries in Livingstone, Zambia at that time. There was no local church when they moved to Zambia in 2010, and the life expectancy in this harsh nation was only thirty-eight years. Demonic depression was prevalent. Orphans were of little concern to that struggling nation. The Bumsteads provided housing and garnered sponsoring support for many orphans through their ministry: Love's Door for all Nations.

Before they returned to the States, the Bumsteads trained a local church planter named Witika Mukale. Since the initial training, many churches have been planted as well as existing churches desiring to connect through the disciple-making movement that has been initiated.

DOVE Zambia has 207 churches actively seeking official partnership through engagement while they continue to reach out and plant churches in villages. This is a slow process due to lack of infrastructure and typical challenges experienced in developing nations. But we are blessed to serve Jesus together with our Zambian brothers and sisters in Christ. Merle and Cheree Shenk, along with Brian and Janet Sauder who serve on the DOVE South Africa Apostolic Council, give spiritual oversight to the DOVE family of leaders in Zambia.

Back to DOVE USA

The sixty-one DOVE USA churches in urban, suburban, and country settings are scattered across Pennsylvania, South Carolina, Kentucky, Virginia, Ohio, Maryland, Texas, New Jersey, Illinois, Michigan, Missouri, Kansas, Connecticut, Massachusetts, New Hampshire, South Dakota, and Oregon.

For ease in interacting with each other, the church leaders connect relationally to other DOVE leaders in one of four regions: Northeast, East Coast, Midwest, and West Coast. Churches within each of these regions gather annually to celebrate God's work in our midst.

Unique outreaches

Ron Myer, DOVE USA director, has often said, "We exist to make Jesus famous and to see His Kingdom expand in and through His people." Although people have different insights and anointings to reach the needs in their spheres of influence, there is no group of believers in any one city, nation, or continent that has a perfect model. We are dependent upon one another to revolutionize every strata of society. This is the true underground church.

You can see from the following examples of how churches uniquely reach out to spread God's love that church is not limited to a specific structure.

- A skate park reaches the youth in Terre Hill, Pennsylvania, led by Craig and Denise Sensenig.

- A local church in Pennsylvania had a passion for their town and began praying for a rundown hotel where over half the police calls originated from. Through a course of God-ordained events, the establishment was purchased by the church, totally remodeled, and today is home for three contemporary for-profit businesses, two of which are owned by the church. Through years of prayer and hard work, they saw this establishment totally transformed from being a detriment to society to being a blessing to the city.

- Churches host five-kilometer runs and fun events such as an Easter egg hunt and harvest festivals. The events are not always evangelistic in nature, but they open doors to develop friendships.

- Joetta Keefer, Hands of Hope director and DOVE missionary, ministers hope and restoration to the homeless in Philadelphia. She organizes hands-on street ministry that touches people at their point of need by providing warm clothing, food, and prayer.

- DOVE Church Wilmington, Ohio, has a close connection with Sugar Tree Ministries who feeds the homeless in their city.

- Island Church in Massachusetts experienced revival when Lee and Teresa DeMatos came to Christ and welcomed neighborhood kids to waterski every weekend. "We don't combine it with a Bible study or say the kids need to come to church. The only rule is we pray before we play," Lee says. The waterskiing events bubble with laughter and fun, and, of course, opportunities pop up. Their neighbors—none of whom had a relationship with God—experienced transformation as they got saved and invited family members. So many got saved that they needed a building. They laid hands on a notorious barroom, claimed it for Jesus and ended up using it as a church building.

These are only a few of the many examples of how DOVE churches in the USA reach out to spread the love of Jesus in their communities.

In 2018 Josh Good joined the staff of DOVE USA as the new youth leader. He says, "We continue to yearn to see the next generation equipped and empowered for Jesus. DOVE USA Youth functions to serve as a resource and encouragement to youth leaders who give of their time in DOVE churches across the States. DOVE USA also creates opportunities for the young people of DOVE to discover who God is, who He says they are, and how God has equipped them to participate in the Kingdom."

For the past 25 years, Evangelistic Missions Training (formerly called Boot Camp) has been a pivotal event in training youth in DOVE. EMT is a week-long immersive experience of teaching, outreach, worship, and prayer for ages 13-19. Josh says, "When I asked a number of young people what their favorite part of EMT was, they didn't say the teachings, they didn't say friendship, they didn't say the worship, and nobody

DOVE USA Youth Evangelism Mission Training (EMT).

even said the food! They unanimously responded, 'Outreach.' Young people do not want to be bystanders of the faith; they want to be on the front lines! They want to pray, they want to prophesy, they want to hear God's voice, and they want to be the hands and feet of Jesus. Sometimes they need some coaxing, or a bit of reminding, but when they are activated by the great love of God, it is a powerful sight!"

CHAPTER 14

Much More to Come!

The Lord continues to take us to new nations and open new doors. We are grateful for these divine connections and Kingdom partnerships. A hallmark of DOVE International is that DOVE churches throughout the world are led by national leaders and not by Americans or by missionary transplants. When DOVE became an international family of churches, God directed us to focus on the vision and biblical values he gave us and not become distracted with smaller things or cultural differences. We major on majors, and minor on minors (Romans 14:5). At the same time, we embrace cultural differences and value what each person and nationality bring to the DOVE International family.

There is a redemptive purpose from God in every culture, and we are blessed to be a family representing so many nations and people groups. We often say, "Our global family of churches is like a pot of stew. Every new church is an ingredient that, when added, makes the stew much 'tastier.'"

My role, along with others on our apostolic team, has been to co-labor with the Lord to build apostolic teams worldwide that oversee and plant churches in their respective nations.

DOVE International Leadership Conference encourages and strengthens the DOVE global family to fulfill the Great Commission.

In many cases, we have led the teams initially until apostolic leaders are trained. For example, I led the DOVE Latin America Apostolic Team for years until Craig Nanna became my assistant. Eventually Craig was affirmed to give leadership to the Latin America team. This team oversees DOVE church leaders in Brazil, Peru, Guatemala, Colombia, and Venezuela. Doug Lehman was mentored for a few years to become the apostolic leader of the DOVE South Central Asia Apostolic Team in 2018.

East Africa has the DOVE Africa Apostolic Team led by Ibrahim and Diane Omondi. Ephraim and Jova Tumusiime and Hesbone and Violet Odindo serve with them on this team. A Kenya apostolic team is led by Hesbone Odindo; a Uganda team is led by Ephraim Tumusiime; a Rwanda apostolic team is led by Levis Kagigi, and a DR Congo team is led by Kitungano Ngoy.

Steve Prokopchak leads the Caribbean team overseeing Barbados, Cuba, and Haiti. Nelson Martin has been overseeing Haiti leaders for many years. Brian Sauder and Lynn Ironside lead the DOVE Canada Apostolic Team. Ron Myer oversees Jeff Hoglen who leads the DOVE Philippines Apostolic Team.

In 2018, Merle and Cheree Shenk and Craig and Tracie Nanna were added to the DOVE International Apostolic Council at our International Leadership Conference. LaVerne and I have been so blessed to serve together with the amazing people on the DOVE International Apostolic Council to pray and plan for the future. It has been a real honor for us to serve alongside many of these leaders for over 35 years. They have become true friends. DOVE International has become a global family of churches and ministries built together by the Holy Spirit and God-given relationships, and united by a common vision and biblical values.

New generations

When LaVerne and I were part of the youth group that reached out to the unchurched in the 1980s, we did not envision starting a church. When our first small group prayed for a name for our fledging church, we had no idea what impact "Declaring Our Victory Emmanuel" would have throughout the nations. Recounting DOVE International's history spurs thankfulness in our hearts for all the Lord has done. Since DOVE's inception, two generations have been birthed. Some of those who were preschoolers when DOVE first began have grown up in the church and birthed a new generation that has also grown up in the church. Many of these have assumed leadership positions. Obviously, not all are called to leadership, but thousands are loyal followers of Jesus.

Recently an elder at one of the DOVE USA churches talked about what it was like growing up in a DOVE church. "We saw miracles, heard prophetic words, and saw God use people. But the greatest impact on me was seeing that it was possible to have a personal relationship with Jesus. Seeing that caused me to study the Word of God, seek Him, and know Him."

It is rewarding to hear and see God's faithfulness through the generations. LaVerne and I are grateful for the Lord's grace upon our four children: Katrina, Charita, Josh and Leticia, who lived out this journey with us. We are proud of each of our children. They shared their parents with people around the world. We know that the other International Apostolic Council members who serve with us and DOVE church leaders worldwide share the same love and devotion for their families. Together, the Lord has given to each of us an amazing inheritance.

Many of us who have lived much of this story find ourselves getting older. We are in the process of discerning the succession for leadership. As Elijah passed on to Elisha a double portion of all the Lord gave to him, we believe the next generation of leaders will experience a double portion of God's grace and blessing. We know God is not finished with the work He began.

We continue to focus on the Lord and on training, releasing, mentoring and protecting the new generations among us as they lead with a double anointing. Together we are preparing the way for the generations to come.

This book is being released during the Covid-19 global pandemic of 2020. Churches throughout the world are currently realizing anew the need to focus on making disciples and experiencing the "under-ground church," small groups of people in relationship with God and each other with a vision to reach their world. Sunday services have been closed to varying degrees worldwide. But the church goes on, from house to house.

The past forty years have been a season for building a strong biblical, relational, and global foundation to prepare us for all the Lord has for the future of the DOVE International family. We do not know what the years ahead hold for the DOVE global family, but we do know this: our God has begun a good work in the hearts of thousands of people around the world. The God who began this good work within each of us will bring it to completion (Philippians 1:6). Throughout the nations we will continue "Declaring Our Victory Emanuel"—God with us—so Jesus can receive all glory and praise.

"Now to him who is able to do immeasurably more
than all we ask or imagine, according to his power
that is at work within us, to him be glory in the church
and in Christ Jesus throughout all generations,
for ever and ever! Amen."

Ephesians 3:20

Things We Learned the Past 40 years

Here are some of the things we learned the past 40 years:

1. God always calls teams to work together.

2. Nothing is more important than having a personal intimate relationship with Jesus.

3. God has been with us so far, and He will be with us in the future.

4. God uses some people in our ministries for a shorter season, and others for a longer season.

5. Never despise the days of small beginnings.

6. Do not assume everyone in your neighborhood knows the Good News about Jesus.

7. Embrace change when it comes.

8. Doing things together with others builds trust and relationships.

9. If God has called you to start a ministry, expect it to multiply.

10. Anyone who knows Jesus can baptize new believers.

11. It is so important for every believer to be connected to a local church.

12. It is healthy to visit various forms of church to develop a love for the body of Christ in its many expressions.

13. Small groups provide opportunities for discipleship and accountability.

14. The underground part of the church is often more important than the part that is above the ground.

15. Our main focus should be making disciples as Jesus taught us, not a Sunday morning church program.

16. Sometimes we need to start a different type of church for new believers and not force them to become part of the present established churches.

17. Jesus taught that new wine (new believers) need new wineskins (new church structures).

18. People also need larger gatherings to hear the word of God preached and to worship corporately.

19. When God speaks, listen and obey.

20. We need to stay hungry for revival and read accounts of past revivals to stir our faith for more.

21. Long term ministry relationships are a great blessing to kingdom expansion. We have been blessed to serve together with many present leaders for more than 35 years.

22. Extraordinary prayer is critical for lasting fruit.

23. Team leadership is critical and every team needs a designated leader.

24. No matter what form of government a church claims to have, there is always one person who openly or quietly holds the greatest influence over the church. Setting up proper government is never a matter of keeping it out of the hands of one person but putting it into the hands of God's person.

25. Servant leadership means each person is valued, no one is above the other, and each is willing to serve wherever needed.

26. When we serve together in unity, our God will command a blessing on us.

27. Let's keep our three main focuses: prayer, evangelism and discipleship.

28. Scriptures affirm that God uses both men and women as leaders. Priscilla and Aquila worked together as a team (Romans 16:3).

29. When we obey the Lord, He will provide for us.

30. New believers must be taught the basic foundations of the Christian life.

31. The most effective leaders come from within – sons and daughters of the house.

32. Churches need a clear plan for evangelism.

33. Pray for two types of people to come to your church: new believers and laborers to help with the harvest.

34. Teaching others does not come natural for most people, they need to be trained to teach.

35. Mentoring a few people at a time will bring amazing results.

36. Finding a balance between ministry and family is essential.

37. Pastors and leaders who are married do not need to die for the church, Jesus already died for the church. Their responsibility is to die for their spouse.

38. Our spouses and families are precious gifts from the Father and need to be a priority.

39. The best gift a man can give his children is to love their mother.

40. Building relationships through hospitality is important.

41. Learn from other ministries. Do not try to reinvent the wheel.

42. Do not fall into the trap of adopting methods that worked for other churches when the Lord had not called you to use those same methods. Do not wear Saul's armor.

43. Having outside accountability is critical for all leaders.

44. All churches need a clear vision.

45. A vital youth ministry is important if we want to be a growing church.

46. It is important to experience the presence of Jesus when we meet together as a church.

47. When someone comes to your church from another church, encourage them to go back to the pastors and leaders of the churches they are leaving and thank and affirm the former church leaders for all that they had sowed into their lives.

48. Sharing commitment to others in a small group should not be seen as legalism, but as a privilege.

49. Everyone needs to be taught about the baptism in the Holy Spirit and learn how to move in the gifts of the Holy Spirit.

50. Children are important to the Lord and wise church leaders find ways to provide ministry to them.

51. New people joining our local church need to go through a biblical foundations course to learn the values of our fellowship so we can be in agreement and serve together effectively.

52. We must stay outward focused, or we become ingrown.

53. Every church needs a connection to the nations to be healthy. International relationships are critical for kingdom advancement.

54. We cannot assume that friends whom we had ministered with and known for many years will be the ones with whom we should build the church.

55. Sending out church planters too soon, before they had fully been immersed in the vision, biblical values and methods of our global church family, can cause problems.

56. Sometimes spiritual seeds that are sown take many years to bring forth a harvest.

57. Working together with the rest of the body of Christ is important and honors the Lord.

58. Growth always requires change.

59. The church is built by relationships, not by geography.

60. Understanding other persons personality profiles helps us serve them better and communicate more effectively. We learn to honor how the Lord has wired them.

61. Prophetic words help prepare us for the future.

62. Prophetic ministry powerfully brings insights and encouragement from God to an individual or group of people.

63. Church leaders today need to be good stewards of all the Lord has given them.

64. If you understand how a healthy family functions, you can understand how a healthy church should operate.

65. We can never allow vision, no matter how good it is, to take the place of Christ's preeminence.

66. We must give proper stewardship to the mantle of leadership the Lord has given to us.

67. The Lord will wash away all of the hurts, expectations, fears, insecurities, and ways of doing things from the past so he can teach us fresh and anew for the future.

68. We must move from a Moses mentality to a Joshua mentality. Moses and the people of God walked "in a circle" for forty years but Joshua had a clear mandate from the Lord to go into the Promised Land. Moses majored on maintenance, Joshua led an army!

69. When you are in leadership and obey God, there will be some "barking dogs" (words spoken, perhaps harshly, against you), but it doesn't matter; the enemy cannot touch you. God knows your heart, and He will vindicate you.

70. Whenever we begin to be too nostalgic, we tend to forget the negative things that have happened and only concentrate on the positive. We need to learn from both victories and mistakes.

71. We must get our significance and security from our relationship with the Lord, not from what we do.

72. We must experience a revelation of our Heavenly Father's love.

73. Pruning in leadership is painful but often necessary for kingdom growth both in our church and in the body of Christ.

74. When you start a ministry, some people are meant to work together short term and some long term. The short-term workers can be compared to the scaffolding and the long-term, the bricks. Both are needed and valued.

75. We all need to become spiritual fathers and mothers and we need to have spiritual fathers and mothers.

76. God speaks through a leader, He speaks through a team, and He speaks through His people.

77. When we acknowledge the Lord in our midst, He will direct our steps.

78. We must make godly decisions that honor the Lord, honor leadership, and honor those whom we serve.

79. Prophetic acts can be really powerful.

80. We must be gripped with the Lord's vision to make disciples after the pattern of Jesus and Paul the apostle.

81. Mentoring only one new disciple each year has the potential to change the world.

82. The Lord will continue to use us even in the midst of pain and struggle if we allow Him to.

83. Sometimes when we ask God to "show us the way" He says: "I am the way."

84. It always pays to walk in God's grace and forgive and receive forgiveness.

85. We need to be in agreement regarding the biblical values that we believe are essential to walk together in unity.

86. Use updated biblical terms for leaders and ministry as the Lord gives more revelation.

87. Sometimes we need to start training others in leadership so others do not make the same mistakes we have made.

88. God uses many different types of churches. We do not have an edge on other churches.

89. Serving in Christian ministry cannot be a career move, but a calling.

90. Only eternity will reveal how many spiritual battles were won around the world because of the obedience of prayer warriors.

91. Our God loves to use unschooled, ordinary men and women who have been with Jesus.

92. We are one small part of the whole body of Christ and privileged to serve with other churches and ministries.

93. We are not called to proselytize or recruit churches or leaders, but we do desire to respond to the Lord when He divinely links us in relationship with churches that have no other spiritual oversight.

94. Everything that has life has the potential to multiply.

95. A focus on missions is critical for kingdom expansion.

96. This world needs as many people as possible—both men and women—who are committed to teaching the truth of God's Word.

97. We value women and what they carry from God.

98. We must count the cost of spreading the gospel, for some of us it may include being martyred for our faith.

99. We walk in obedience and faith, not always knowing how God is working behind the scenes or how He is guiding our paths.

100. Starting new spiritual families is the most effective way to see people come to faith in Christ.

101. In parts of the world facing persecution, we must be careful to not communicate anything on social media about them that would place our brothers and sisters in danger.

102. We believe God uses micro churches, community churches and megachurches. The important thing is not the structure, but whether discipleship is happening.

103. Our God uses divine connections and kingdom partnerships to build his kingdom globally.

104. We look forward to the coming years, transitioning leadership to a younger generation of leaders who will take the DOVE family far ahead of anything we have experienced thus far.

105. We have been so blessed and are eternally grateful for every person who has been willing to serve with us. In times of abundance and in the hard times, we experienced the Lord's grace and His great blessing again and again.

DOVE Family Churches

Global Locations

DOVE International churches are located in many nations. For more details visit www.dcfi.org.

Africa

Democratic Republic of Congo
Kenya
Mozambique
Rwanda
Tanzania
Uganda
South Africa
Zambia

Asia/South Pacific

Myanmar
Philippines
Three nations in South Central Asia
(Names withheld because of possible persecution.)

Caribbean

Barbados
Cuba
Haiti

Europe

Bulgaria
Denmark
Scotland
The Netherlands

Latin America

Brazil
Colombia
Guatemala
Peru
Venezuela

North America

Canada
United States of America

Our Values

All values and guiding principles for the DOVE International family must be rooted in the Scriptures (II Tim. 3:16-17, II Tim. 2:15).

1. Knowing God the Father through His Son Jesus Christ and living by His Word is the foundation of life.

We believe that the basis of the Christian faith is to know God through repentance for sin, receiving Jesus Christ as Lord, building an intimate relationship with Him and being conformed into His image. God has declared us righteous through faith in Jesus Christ (John 1:12, John 17:3, Rom. 8:29, II Cor. 5:21).

2. It is essential for every believer to be baptized with the Holy Spirit and be completely dependent on Him.

We recognize that we desperately need the person, presence and power of the Holy Spirit to minister effectively in our generation. Changed lives are not the product of men's wisdom, but of the demonstration of the power of the Holy Spirit as modeled in the New Testament (I Cor. 2:2-5, John 15:5). We believe it is essential for every believer to be baptized with the Holy Spirit and to pursue spiritual gifts (Luke 3:16, Acts 1:8, II Cor. 13:14, John 4:23-24).

All decisions need to be made by listening to the Holy Spirit as we make prayer a priority and learn to be worshippers. Worship helps us focus on the Lord and allows us to hear His voice more clearly.

We recognize that we do not wrestle against flesh and blood, but against demonic forces. Jesus Christ is our Lord, our savior, our healer and our deliverer (Eph. 6:12, I John 3:8).

3. The Great Commission will be completed through prayer, evangelism, discipleship and church planting.

We are committed to helping fulfill the Great Commission through prayer and fasting, evangelism, discipleship and church planting locally, nationally and internationally in order to reach both Jew and Gentile (Matt. 28:19-20, Matt. 6:5-18, Acts 1:8). We believe water baptism is essential for those who have chosen to follow Christ (Acts 2:38, Rom. 6:4, Gal. 3:27).

We are called to support other co-laborers as churches are planted throughout the world. The Great Commission is fulfilled through tearing down spiritual strongholds of darkness and planting churches (I Cor. 3:6-9, Matt. 11:12, II Cor. 10:3-4, Acts 14:21-23).

We are also called to proclaim the gospel through the arts, publications, and the media and trust that God will continue to raise up other resources and ministries to assist us in extending His kingdom (I Cor. 9:19-22).

4. We deeply value the sacred covenant of marriage and the importance of training our children to know Christ.

It is our belief God gives the gift of single life to some, and the gift of married life to others, all within the standard of holiness and purity (I Cor. 7). We believe marriage is between one man and one woman. Both marriage and family are instituted by God, and healthy, stable families are essential for the church to be effective in fulfilling its mission. Parents are called by God to walk in the character of Christ and to train their children in the nurture and loving discipline of the Lord (Mark 10:6-8, Eph. 5:22-6:4).

The Lord is calling His people to walk in the fear of the Lord and in a biblical standard of holiness and purity. The covenant of marriage is ordained by God and needs to be honored and kept (Prov. 16:6, Mark 10:9, I Thess. 4:3-8, I Cor. 6:18-20).

5. We are committed to spiritual families, spiritual parenting and intergenerational connections.

Believing that our God is turning the hearts of the fathers and mothers to the sons and daughters in our day, we are committed to spiritual parenting on every level of ministry and church life (Mal. 4:5-6, I Cor. 4:15-17).

Participation in a small group or house church is fundamental to commitment to the DOVE family. The small group is a group of believers and/or families who are committed to one another and to reach others for Christ. We believe the Lord desires to raise up spiritual families in many levels including small groups, house churches, congregations, apostolic movements and the kingdom of God (I Cor. 12:18, Eph. 4:16).

We believe each spiritual family needs to share common values, vision, goals and a commitment to build together, and needs to receive ongoing training in these areas (Ps. 133, II Pet. 1:12-13, II Tim. 2:2).

We are committed to reaching, training and releasing young people as co-laborers for the harvest, as the young and the old labor together (Acts 2:17, Jer. 31:13).

6. Spiritual multiplication and reproduction must extend to every sphere of kingdom life and ministry.

Multiplication is expected and encouraged in every sphere of church life. Small groups should multiply into new small groups and churches should multiply into new churches. Church planting must be a goal of every congregation (Acts 9:31, Mark 4:20).

The DOVE family of churches will be made up of many new regional families of churches as apostolic fathers and mothers are released in the nations and regions of the world (Acts 11:19-30, Acts 13-15).

7. Relationships are essential in building God's kingdom.

Serving others and building trust and relationships are desired in every area of church life. We believe the best place to begin to serve and experience trust and relationship is in some type of small group experience (Acts 2:42-47, Eph. 4:16, Gal. 5:13).

We are joined together primarily by God-given family relationships, not by organization, hierarchy, or bureaucracy (I Pet. 2:5).

8. Every Christian is both a priest and a minister.

We believe that the work of ministry belongs not to a select few, but is the responsibility of every believer. Every Christian is a priest who needs to minister to the Lord, hear from the Lord personally and minister to others (I Pet. 2:9, Rev. 1:5-6). This ministry starts in the home, which is a center for ministry.

Fivefold ministers are the Lord's gifts to His church. He uses fivefold persons to help equip each believer to become an effective minister in order to build up the body of Christ (Eph. 4:11-12).

9. A servant's heart is necessary for every leader to empower others.

We believe every sphere of leadership needs to include a clear servant-leader called by God and a team who is called to walk together. The leader has the anointing and responsibility to discern the mind of the Lord that is expressed through the leadership team (II Cor. 10:13-16, Num. 27:16, I Pet. 5:1-4).

Leaders are called to listen to what the Lord is saying through those whom they serve as they model servant-leadership. They are called to walk in humility and integrity, in the fruit of the Spirit, and in the fear of the Lord (Acts 6:2-6, Acts 15, Matt. 20:26, Gal. 5:22-23).

We believe God raises up both apostolic overseers and partner church elders to direct, protect, correct and discipline the church.

These leaders must model the biblical qualifications for leadership (Acts 15, Acts 6:1-4, I Tim. 3, Titus 1).

Leaders must purpose to equip, empower and release others, thereby encouraging every individual to fulfill his or her call from the Lord (Titus 1:5, I Tim 4:12-14). Those with other spiritual gifts—including administrative gifts—need to be released to serve on every level of church life (I Cor. 12).

We believe that we all need to submit to those who rule over us in the Lord and esteem them highly in love for their work's sake (Heb. 13:17, I Thess. 5:12-13).

10. Biblical prosperity, generosity and integrity are essential to kingdom expansion.

Biblical prosperity is God's plan to help fulfill the Great Commission. The principle of the tithe is part of God's plan to honor and provide substance for those He has placed over us in spiritual authority. Those who are over us in the Lord are responsible for the proper distribution of the tithes and offerings (III John 2, Matt. 23:23, Heb. 7:4-7, Mal. 3:8-11, Acts 11:29-30).

We believe in generously giving offerings to support individuals, churches and ministries both inside and outside of the DOVE family. We encourage individuals, small groups, congregations and ministries to support fivefold ministers and missionaries in both prayer and finances (II Cor. 8:1-7, Gal. 6:6, Phil. 4:15-17).

We believe that every area of ministry and church life needs to be financially responsible and accountable to those giving them oversight in order to maintain a high standard of integrity. Spiritual leaders receiving a salary from the church are discouraged from setting their own salary level (Gal. 6:5, Rom. 15:14, I Thess. 5:22, II Cor. 8:20-21).

11. The gospel compels us to send missionaries to the un-reached and help those least able to meet their own needs.

Jesus instructs us to take the gospel to the ends of the earth. Our mission is to reach the unreached areas of the world with the gospel of Jesus Christ by sending trained missionaries and through church planting. Together we join with the body of Christ to reach the unreached (Matt. 24:14, Acts 1:8, Acts 13:1-4, II Cor. 10:15-16).

We are also called to help the poor and needy, those in prison, orphans and widows. This includes local, national and international outreach. When we help the poor, both materially and spiritually, we are lending to the Lord (Deut. 14:28-29, Deut. 26:10-12, Matt. 25:31-46, James 1:27, Prov. 19:17).

12. We are called to build the kingdom together with the entire body of Christ.

Our focus is on the kingdom of God, recognizing our small group, our local church and DOVE International as just one small part of God's kingdom. We are called to link together with other groups in the body of Christ and pursue unity in His church as we reach the world together (Matt. 6:33, Eph. 4:1-6, John 17, Ps. 133).

We wish to see God's kingdom come not just in and through the church, but in all areas of life. Therefore, we are called to minister in the church, the family, government, the arts, education, business and the media, so that all such spheres come under the Lordship of Jesus Christ and reflect the values of His kingdom (Matt. 6:10).

We believe in utilizing and sharing the human and material resources the Lord has blessed us with. This includes the fivefold ministry, missions, leadership training and other resources the Lord has entrusted to us (I Cor. 12, Acts 2:44-45).

Our unifying focus is on Christ, His Word and the Great Commission, and we believe we should not be distracted by minor differences (Romans 14:5). We recognize and honor the redemptive purpose of God found in many cultures and ethnicities (Rev. 5:9-10).

The Scriptures serve as a light to guide us, and our Statement of Faith and these values and guiding principles unite us as partner churches. Along with many churches and ministries, we also accept the Lausanne Covenant as a broad statement of evangelical belief. (Matt. 28:19-20, Amos 3:3, I Cor. 1:10, I Cor 15:10).

DOVE International Apostolic Council Team

We have been so honored and blessed to serve together with the many leaders who have labored with us over the past 40 years. Some have served short term, and others have served long term. We are eternally grateful for each person who has served the DOVE International family. Below is the present DOVE International Apostolic Council team.

Larry and
LaVerne Kreider

Ron and Bonnie
Myer

Peter and
Ruth Ann Bunton

Craig and
Tracie Nanna

Hesbone and
Violet Odindo

Ibrahim and
Diane Omondi

Steve and
Mary Prokopchak

Brian and
Janet Sauder

Merle and
Cheree Shenk

House to House

The church is waking up to the simple, successful house to house strategy practiced by the New Testament church. *House to House* documents how God called a fellowship of believers to become a house to house movement. During the past years, DOVE International has grown into a family of small group based churches and micro churches networking throughout the world. *By Larry Kreider, 264 pages.* **$15.99**

The Cry for Spiritual Mothers and Fathers

Returning to the biblical truth of spiritual parenting so believers are not left fatherless and disconnected. How loving, seasoned spiritual fathers and mothers help spiritual children reach their full potential in Christ.
By Larry Kreider, 224 pages. **$14.99**

The Biblical Role of Elders for Today's Church

Healthy leadership teams produce healthy churches! New Testament principles for equipping church leadership teams: What are the qualifications and responsibilities, how elders should be chosen, how elders function as spiritual fathers and mothers, how elders should make decisions, resolve conflicts and more. *By Larry Kreider, Ron Myer, Steve Prokopchak, and Brian Sauder, 274 pages.* **$12.99**

Micro Church Networks

Discover how micro church networks offer community and simplicity, especially as they fit the heart, call and passion of the younger generations. These micro church networks work together with the more traditional community churches and megachurches to show the transforming power of Christ to our neighborhoods. *By Larry Kreider, 206 pages:* **$12.99**

MANY DISCOUNTS!

DOVE Store   1.800.848.5892
www.store.dcfi.org

BIBLICAL FOUNDATIONS FOR LIFE

Presented by Larry Kreider

Sign up to receive our *FREE* 365 Day Devotional Video Series

Scan the QR Code with your mobile device's camera, or go to dcfi.org/devos

BIBLICAL
FOUNDATIONS
FOR LIFE

BROUGHT TO YOU BY DOVE INTERNATIONAL

Biblical Foundation Series

This series by Larry Kreider covers basic Christian doctrine. Practical illustrations accompany the easy-to-understand format. Use for small group teachings (48 in all), a mentoring relationship or daily devotional. Each book has 64 pages: **$5.99** each, 12 Book Set: **$39** Also available in Spanish and French.

Biblical Foundation Titles
1. Knowing Jesus Christ as Lord
2. The New Way of Living
3. New Testament Baptisms
4. Building For Eternity
5. Living in the Grace of God
6. Freedom from the Curse
7. Learning to Fellowship with God
8. What is the Church?
9. Authority and Accountability
10. God's Perspective on Finances
11. Called to Minister
12. The Great Commission

A Practical Path to a Prosperous Life

A clear biblical, step-by-step approach to attaining abundant personal finances, building wealth and financing of the Great Commission in our day. Age-old biblical truths with practical, present-day applications to help your thinking line up with the God's Word. By Brian Sauder, *282 pages:* **$12.99**

Building Your Personal House of Prayer

Christians often struggle with their prayer lives. With the unique "house plan" developed in this book, each room corresponding to a part of the Lord's Prayer, your prayer life is destined to go from duty to joy! Includes a helpful Daily Prayer Guide to use each day.
by Larry Kreider, 254 pages: **$15.99**

Fivefold Ministry

Discover how the fivefold ministry was created to work within the local church, the training ground for ministry. These ministers–apostles, prophets, evangelists, pastors and teachers–are coaches who equip and train God's people for works of service. Find out what the fivefold ministry is and what it is not as we learn how proven ministers can be released in the body of Christ. *By Ron Myer, 208 pages:* **$15.99**

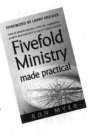

Straight Talk to Leaders

What we wish we had known when we started. Four Christian leaders disclose key leadership lessons they have learned through forty years of pastoring and establishing worldwide ministries. This illuminating book explores topics such as team building, boundaries, transitions, unity, stress management, learning from criticism, making tough decisions and much more! *By Larry Kreider, Sam Smucker, Barry Wissler and Lester Zimmerman, 204 pages:* **$12.99**

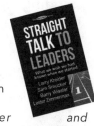

and

Passing the 21 Tests of Leadership

Whether you are called to lead in business, your community or church, life is filled with tests! Will you be able to pass them? *"I encourage every believer who desires to reach his or her maximum leadership potential to invest in this book." - Robert Stearns, Eagles' Wings Ministries. By Larry Kreider, 218 pages:* **$16.99**

Called Together Pre and postmarital workbook

This unique workbook, specifically designed for couple-to-couple mentoring use, prepares couples for a successful and God-honoring marriage. *Called Together* supplies down-to-earth Biblical wisdom to help couples get off to a positive start. Includes postmarital checkups at three and nine months. Special sections for remarriage, intercultural marriages and remarriages of senior adults. *By Steve and Mary Prokopchak, 250 pages:* **$19.99**

When God Seems Silent

Discovering His purposes in times of confusion and darkness Why does it sometimes feel like God is silent? Is He hiding from us? Is He angry? Larry and LaVerne Kreider help us examine these questions and many of the barriers that can block the voice of God in our lives. They also reveal their own struggle with God's silences and the tremendous breakthroughs that can be discovered. *By Larry and LaVerne Kreider, 208 pages:* **$12.99**

Finding Freedom

Becoming whole and living free The struggle is real. We desire to follow Christ, but too often we find ourselves entangled and tripped up, falling back into the old patterns of our former selves. Authors examine God's Word for the answers and share from their own lives and others who have experienced God's true freedom. *By Larry Kreider, Craig and Tracie Nanna 198 pages:* **$12.99**

Encountering the Supernatural

Discover God's amazing power and prescene in your life Wherever you are in your spiritual journey, this book will place you on a path to greater revelation of God's supernatural power in everyday life. *By Larry Kreider, Kevin Kazemi and Merle Shenk,* 220 pages: **$12.09**

Battle Cry for Your Marriage

Discovering breakthroughs for today's challenges With raw honesty four couples tackle issues of spiritual, emotional and sexual intimacy along with other marital stresses. Biblically-based insights will inspire spouses to face issues, communicate honestly, find life-changing strategies and—most of all—love the One who gave them the gift of each other.
By Larry and LaVerne Kreider, Steve and Mary Prokopchak Duane and Reyna Britton, Wallace and Linda Mitchell, 204 pages: **$12.99**